RELIGION *VS* JESUS
DO *VS* DONE

Explanation of scripture the "religious"
use to deny salvation by grace alone

PRESTON GREENE

PRESS

Dedication Page

———∽∽∽———

1. To my God, Who took all the ordinances against me and nailed them to His cross. For simply offering me Salvation as a free gift, by grace. For answering my prayer. If He hadn't answered my prayer, I would still be confused.

2. To my parents. I was away from the Bible for 20 years. God hit me over the head with a "ton of bricks". When He did, all I could remember was, "Jesus is the Way, the Truth and the Life". That's a good place to start! It was hammered into my head during my youth.

3. To my wife, who, during a 4-5 year period when I studied (searched) for truth for about 4,000 hours, NEVER complained to me about helping around the house or spending more time with her. To this day, when discussing the Bible with many on the web, she still does not complain.

4. To all those who helped in my walk to find truth. The list is too long to name everyone. However, God KNOWS who you are!

Contents

———✦✦✦———

Chapter 1 – My Walk, a Brief Overview 7

Chapter 2 – The Gospel. 14

Chapter 3 – What does it mean to believe? 18

Chapter 4 – Eternal Security 21

Chapter 5 – Hebrews 6:4-6 29

Chapter 6 – Hebrews 10:26 34

Chapter 7 – Can I be cast away? 41

Chapter 8 – Faith without works is dead – James 2 44

Chapter 9 – Even the devils believe and tremble 49

Chapter 10 – Repent of your sins? 55

Chapter 11 – Meaning of the word "Repent" 66

Chapter 12 – I never knew you. 70

Chapter 13 – 1 John 3:9. 75

Chapter 14 – The "Lists" 81

Chapter 15 – Fruit Inspectors 86

Chapter 16 – Examine yourself. 95

Chapter 17 – Go and sin no more. 98

Chapter 18 – Is Water Baptism a "requirement"? 101

Chapter 19 – Roman Catholicism and its doctrine 108

Chapter 20 – Some random verses 117

Chapter 21 – SHOULD do 121

Chapter 22 – Elected? 125

Chapter 23 – Why the Bible? 133

Chapter 24 – The Gospel revisited 140

Chapter 25 – Conclusion 145

Chapter 1

My walk, a brief overview

In 2009, God hit me over the head with what felt like a ton of bricks. I won't get into the story, but He certainly got my attention. When I awoke from the knockout, I remembered one thing from my youth. It was: "Jesus is the way, truth and the life." I thought, "Time to get back to my Bible." When I finally found it, it took a while to remove all the dust it had collected over the past 20 years, but I was ready to roll. I picked it up and started to read it. I **KNEW** that my reading comprehension was not that good as my SAT scores on the verbal section clearly showed I should have been in the 5th grade. As a result of this poor confidence, I would use the internet to help me find the truth and the meaning of certain passages. Needless to say, my confusion level rose to 8 out of 10. There were so many interpretations of scripture; so many different gospels and how to get to heaven. Although I was confused, I didn't let it get to me. I would stick with the Bible and continue to try to find truth. This was my walk with God and nobody else's. As a result, I didn't go to specific people for answers.

After a while, pure panic set in. I wasn't sure how to go to heaven when I died. I **KNEW** there were a heaven and a hell. I **KNEW** I didn't want to go to hell. Couldn't I just be annihilated? One moment I would read about grace. The next moment I would read about Jesus telling me, "I never knew you." I began to panic even more. I didn't understand. How could the Bible say grace in one place then say "be ye perfect" in another? How could Jesus promise to lose nothing while Hebrews 6 seemed to read that I could lose my salvation? How could Paul say "salvation without works" while James seemed to contradict it? How could the Bible say we are saved without the law then say, "do these sins and you won't inherit the kingdom of God"? Was water baptism a requirement? What a roller coaster ride. One day I thought I was saved and filled with joy. The next day I would panic because of a new scripture that I read and couldn't understand.

Like most "logical" people, I thought, "I need to try to stop as much sinning as I can, just in case." You know, trusting the other JC (Justin Case). So I began to attempt to stop as many sins as I could—even smoking. You know... just-in-case I needed to. I tried. God knows I tried. The fear of hell can do that to a person, ya know! To make a long story short, I couldn't stop my sinning. After seven weeks, I started to smoke again. YES, I craved it more after seven weeks. YES, my wife irritated me that much on that day. IF you have a wife, you **KNOW** what I mean (love you, dear!). All I could think was... "**FAILURE**". How humiliating. I could be going to hell and I can't stop smoking. How could I not stop doing something, knowing it could possibly send me to hell? Now my panic level was a 19 on a scale of 1-10. The panic got so bad, I was considering cutting off a hand or plucking out an eye

(Matt 5:29); surgically removed of course. You know, just to show God I was serious. That's pure panic! I prayed to God, "What's the point? I can't live it. If I am going to hell anyway, I should not be a Christian and live it up while I still can."

There was still a part of me that couldn't let go. Saying that prayer, I ended with, "Where's the REST you promised me? I have no REST." I went to bed and woke up the next morning. And guess what? **NO PANIC**. I still couldn't explain all those "difficult" verses , *but* the panic and fear were gone. I first thought, "That's kinda amazing." THEN I thought, "God answered my prayer!" WOW. He actually heard me and did something about my problem. That was simply... cool! A prayer being answered by God is almost as good as it gets. Well, approximately a year later, I was STILL confused on certain passages of scripture. I mean, the biggest thing that hindered my faith at this point was the Bible. YEP, I said it! The Bible! I kept saying to God, "Why is this book so hard to understand?" Nevertheless, I kept at it. I was getting **nowhere** real fast. My frustration level grew to a level I had only ever seen from my wife when the kids would run across the carpet with their muddy shoes. I was angry.

After two years and 2,000 hours of study, I felt just as stupid as I did the previous year. I mean, really? Who studies THAT much with little to no results? One day, still being very angry, I decided to read James for the tenth time to see if I could "figure it out". I didn't get very far.

> "If any of you lack wisdom, let him ask of God, that giveth to all men liberally, and upbraideth not; and it shall be given him. But let him ask in faith, nothing wavering" (James 1:5,6).

That sounded like a promise to me. Then it hit me. I immediately went to my prayer spot and my prayer went something like this (remember, I was angry):

"Dear God, I am mad—very mad. I don't understand this book and it is **YOUR** fault. Why did you make this book too hard to understand OR why did you make me too stupid to understand it? Either way, it's **YOUR** fault. All I ever wanted was the truth. Is that so bad? You know—the simple truth. All this studying and I am no closer to the real truth. Well God, I just read that if I asked you for knowledge, you will give it to me. That sounded like a promise. God, I **DEMAND** that you keep your promise and give me knowledge. You are God and **you can't lie**. You promised it so I **expect** you to keep your promise." Then a little voice asked, "Are you wavering?" I thought for a few seconds as I began to remember who it was I was talking to. I replied, "**NO**! I am not wavering, God promised and I **expect Him** to deliver on it! In Jesus's name, amen."

For those of you who think I would get hit with a lightning bolt because of this prayer, I can assure you that I have not been struck. I think God was smiling at me. I could see Him saying, "It's about time you put your faith in one of my promises!" Let me tell you—the flood gates opened and my eyes began to see. I was getting answers from everywhere. Not only was I getting answers, but they were coming quickly. It was amazing. To this day, this is the most productive prayer I have ever prayed. After getting the answers I needed, I was ready. I was ready to go out and "contend for the faith" (Jude

10

1:3). I was ready to take on "religion". Bring them on. Bring on all the "Goliaths" of religion. I will stand as David with my sling (my KJV1611). It quickly became apparent to me that "religion" had its tentacles around much of professing Christianity. I quickly learned that the gospel was under attack from just about **EVERY** denomination. I also realized, no matter how much scripture I knew, people had problems believing that salvation was truly by grace without works (Rom 11:6, Eph 2:8-9, Rom 4:5-6).

Most believed you had to do "something" or "stop doing something" to go to heaven. They would always bring up passages. I would always explain those passages using other scripture to support my claims. **NOTHING!** I was getting very little results for my contending. Well, back to the Internet with more discussions with the "religious"; I was starting to see some results. Not many results, but some cases where I could see I had helped someone. I would debate with the "sinless perfectionists". You know them. They are the ones who don't sin anymore; their gospel is "go and sin no more" (yes, I will explain that passage later in the book). They could **NEVER** answer my questions, but I could answer most of theirs. I never got one of these "sinless perfectionists" to believe the real gospel. However, others would read the "thread" and email me.

Preston, those answers were great. I would have never been able to answer like that. Thank you. I am going to go home and study them.
Preston, I am not sure I am going to heaven. Can you help me?
Preston, what about this passage? Can you explain it?

I felt great. I felt like I was "in the fight". I felt **HUMBLE**. Wow. God can use a sinner like me to contribute. I thought, "Without that prayer and without God keeping His promise to give me knowledge, I couldn't do any of this." I looked back three years and pondered, "Look how far I have come. Look at what I have been through. Look at how I have separated from religion. Look at me contending for the faith." Three years prior, I would be shot gunning a beer with my kids taping it and uploading it to their MySpace page. I was the "cool" parent (to other kids). I was considered one of the top soccer coaches in the community and I could down a beer in two seconds. Somewhere along the lines, my priorities seemed to change. I was helping a young man recently with some passages of scripture. He made the comment, "You should write a book. That would be helpful." I thought, "Who would buy it? There would be no point if nobody purchased it!" I am not a big author. Then I thought, "The **BIGGEST** event in my life was God's answer to my prayer to give me knowledge." Once I could figure out those passages that "religion" used to deny salvation by grace through faith in the gospel **ALONE**, my faith grew.

If God wants to use my book, it is HIS choice to use it. So, here it is—a book that will go through MANY (not all) of these passages. We will use scripture to explain scripture. We shall see, without a doubt, that salvation is **100% FREE** apart from any works as well as knowing once you are saved, you are eternally secure. Did I mention salvation is absolutely **FREE?!** I claim no specific denomination. I am neither a Calvinist nor an Arminian. I am a Bible-ist, **KJV PREFERRED**. So pick up your Bible and walk with me through all the scriptures used in this book. Be a good berean and verify its claims. This book is built upon scripture. Many verses are listed in parenthesis along with the passages quoted as scripture is used to support scripture. If you look up every passage, you should have some good "markings" in your Bible.

ALL SCRIPTURE IS TAKEN FROM THE KJV.

I hope you enjoy the ride.

For your first exercise; go grab a pen and a piece of paper. Yep, do not read any further until you have something to write with and something to write onto. Next, I need you to write your answer down to these two questions.

1. Do you know for sure where you are going when you die?
2. Why or why not?

Once you have answered these two questions, it is time to move forward to Chapter 2.

Chapter 2

The Gospel

—✐✐✐—

This book will start and end with the gospel. The verses presented here are **CLEAR**. They can't possibly be taken to mean "something else". The Bible, being the word of God **CANNOT** contradict itself.

"For I am not ashamed of the GOSPEL of Christ: for it is the power of God unto salvation to everyone that BELIEVETH" (Romans 1:16).

So what is the gospel according to the Bible? I mean, since IT IS the power of God unto salvation to whoever believes it. The gospel is DECLARED in 1 Corinthians.

"Moreover, brethren, I **DECLARE** unto you the **GOSPEL** which I preached unto you, which also ye have received, and wherein ye stand; By which also ye are saved......how that **Christ DIED FOR OUR SINS** according to the scriptures; and that he was buried, and that he rose again the third day according to the scriptures" (1 Corinthians 15:1,2,4).

So what happens when someone believes/trusts that Jesus (God in the flesh) **DIED FOR OUR SINS** and rose from the dead? The answer is in Ephesians.

"In whom ye also **TRUSTED**, after that ye heard the word of truth, the **GOSPEL** of your salvation: in whom also after that ye **BELIEVED**, ye were **SEALED** with that Holy Spirit of promise" (Eph 1:13).

We see that when people believe (put TOTAL confidence in; trust; rely upon) this GOSPEL—that Jesus "died for **THEIR** sins"—they are SEALED by the Holy Spirit. One can never be unsealed. One is sealed until the day of redemption.

"...and grieve not the Holy Spirit whereby **YE ARE SEALED** unto the day of redemption" (Eph 4:30).

Simply to clarify from a different angle—how many sins did Jesus die for (pay for)? The Bible is clear. Jesus died for **ALL** of them.

"And you, being dead in your sins and the uncircumcision of your flesh, hath he quickened together with him, having **FORGIVEN YOU ALL TRESPASSES**; Blotting out the handwriting of ordinances that was against us, which was contrary to us, and took it out of the way, nailing it to his cross" (Col 2:13,14).

"And by him all that **believe** are justified from **ALL THINGS**, from which ye could not be justified by the law of Moses" (Acts 13:39).

Okay—there should be no question as to what these verses mean. It's pretty clear. They can't be taken any other way. Now I would like to translate this into a worldly example. This has helped others in the past.

"For the wages of sin is death, but the **GIFT** of God is eternal life through Jesus Christ our Lord" (Romans 6:23).

This verse is sending two clear messages. First, notice salvation is a GIFT. Pssssst, a little secret for you: Gifts are free! Second is what we owe for our sin. "Wages" is a term mostly used for employment. Wages are what are owed to the employee in exchange for the work they have done. Well, death is what we owe in exchange for our sin. Death, in this passage, can be referring to physical death or to the second death, which is eternal torment in a literal lake of fire (See Rev 20:14). Both can apply. "The wages of sin is death." So, let's ask ourselves a few questions, shall we?

1. If you had 10 chocolate bars and you gave away ALL 10 bars, how many bars would you have left? The answer: **NONE**.
2. If you had 25 mugs at a yard sale and someone bought ALL 25 mugs, how many mugs would you have left? The answer: **NONE**
3. If you had $100 and a thief stole ALL $100, how many dollars would you have left? The answer: **NONE**

HERE IT COMES!

4. If you have ALL these sins you owe as wages and JESUS came and paid for ALL those sins, how many sins would you have left to send you to hell? The answer: **NONE**.

Yes, it is that simple. Jesus died to pay for **ALL** your sins. This is the gospel (the good news). All you must do is believe it. The moment you do, you are sealed by the Holy Spirit unto the day of redemption. IF you have not truly trusted Him yet, would you trust Him now? **DON'T** trust religion, works, the law, sacraments, church affiliation, etc. **DO TRUST** (believe; put your faith in) the gospel.

Chapter 3

What does it mean to "believe"?

—◦◦◦—

The word "believe" has got to be one of the most mis-understood words of all time. It is probably second only to the word "repent". What does it mean to believe in Jesus? This is what we will define in this brief chapter. How important is belief when it comes to salvation? Well, let's look at some words from Jesus himself.

- JESUS SAID—That whosoever **BELIEVETH in him** should not perish, but HAVE eternal life (John 3:15)
- JESUS SAID—For God so loved the world, that he gave his only begotten Son, that whosoever **BELIEVETH in him** should not perish, but HAVE everlasting life (John 3:16)
- JESUS SAID—He that **BELIEVETH on him** is NOT con-demned: but he that believeth not is condemned already, because he hath not believed in the name of the only begotten Son of God (John 3:18)
- JESUS SAID—Verily, verily, I say unto you, He that heareth my word, and **BELIEVETH on him** that sent me, HATH everlasting life, and shall not come into

condemnation; but is passed from death unto life. (John 5:24)

- JESUS SAID–Jesus answered and said unto them, This is the work of God, that ye **BELIEVE on him** whom he hath sent. (John 6:29)

- JESUS SAID–And Jesus said unto them, I am the bread of life: he that cometh to me shall never hunger; and he **that BELIEVETH on me** shall **NEVER** thirst (John 6:35)

- JESUS SAID–And this is the will of him that sent me, that every one which seeth the Son, **and BELIEVETH on him**, may HAVE everlasting life: and I will raise him up at the last day (John 6:40)

- JESUS SAID–Verily, verily, I say unto you, He that **BELIEVETH** on me HATH everlasting life (John 6:47)

- JESUS SAID–He that **BELIEVETH on me**, as the scripture hath said, out of his belly shall flow rivers of LIVING water. (John 7:38)

- JESUS SAID–Jesus said unto her, I am the resurrection, and the life: he that **BELIEVETH in me**, though he were dead, yet shall he LIVE: (John 11:25)

I really don't think we need any more examples, do you? Believe is it. However, we're back to the original question: what does it mean to believe? I asked myself this question once. I decided to go to Strong's Concordance. This is the definition...

Word: *pisteuw*

1) to have faith in, to be persuaded of, to credit, place confidence in
   1a) of the thing believed
   1a1) to credit, **have confidence**
   1b) in a moral or religious reference
2) by implication, to commit or entrust, i.e. to entrust your spiritual well-being **to Christ**
   2a) to make a commitment (**to trust**)
   2b) to put in **trust** with or **place confidence in**

We can pretty much conclude that believe means **"to trust, to put confidence in"**. Now, go back and **re-read** those verses from Jesus. Substitute "believe" with "to trust, to put confidence in".

The problem today is that most professing Christians are **NOT** trusting in Jesus for their salvation. They are trusting in everything **BUT** Jesus to go to heaven—things like works, law, sacraments, church attendance, tithing, etc. Their faith is **NOT** in Jesus. Escaping eternal damnation rests solely on whom or what a person's faith is in! MOST are putting their faith, their trust, and their confidence in **THEMSELVES** to be "good enough" to make it. Hopefully, this is not you. Look at what Jesus said over and over again.

This is why I **HATE** religion! Have you believed (trusted) in Jesus and the gospel yet? Are you *truly* putting your faith in Jesus **ALONE** to save you?

Chapter 4

Eternal Security

—⌇⌇⌇—

E ternal security is **PREVELANT** in the scriptures. If one does not believe in eternal security, then he or she saying, in effect, "I have to do something to obtain it or keep it." This results in NOT BELIEVING (putting total confidence in) the gospel and putting SOME amount of confidence in his or her self. Below are ten reasons why I believe in the eternal security of the believer. Always remember, the Bible CANNOT contradict itself.

Reason 1 – Everlasting life means everlasting life. In the book of John, the words "eternal life" are directly correlated with believe. (See last chapter). Take John 6:47,

"Verily, verily I say unto thee, he that believeth in me HATH everlasting life.

The word "hath" is present tense; similar to "has". A person who put his or her full trust (believes) in Jesus HAS everlasting life. If one HAS everlasting life, how long does it last? It lasts forever. *If one could lose his or her salvation, then the person never had everlasting life.* They had temporary life. Thus Jesus would have lied and that is impossible.

In hope of eternal life, which God, that **CANNOT** lie, **promised** before the world began (Titus 1:2)

Reason 2 – Sealed means sealed. As we have seen in the chapter, "The Gospel", one is sealed the moment he or she believes (trusts) the Gospel. We also have seen that this person is "sealed" unto the day of redemption (Eph 4:30). If a person is sealed unto the day of redemption, how can one lose salvation? People are either sealed unto the day of redemption or they are not sealed unto the day of redemption. Since the Bible is the word of God, I will believe (Eph 4:30).

Reason 3 – Jesus promised to lose nothing in the book of John.

"For I came down from heaven, not to do mine own will, but the will of him that sent me.

"And this is the Father's will which hath sent me, that of all which he hath given me **I SHOULD LOSE NOTHING**, but should raise it up again at the last day. And this is the will of him that sent me, that every one which seeth the Son, and believeth on him, may have everlasting life: and I will raise him up at the last day" (John 6:39,40).

Are we to think that when Jesus has one, He will actually lose one? I see the "should". However, since Jesus is God (I Tim 3:16; John 1:14), are we to think that He will lose one?

Reason 4 – The Bible states that ALL sins are forgiven to the believer. ALL in the Greek is PAZ–it means total, all, 100%, always (which is a measure of time). If the Bible says ALL my sins are forgiven (past, present, future) then I CAN'T lose my salvation.

"And you, being dead in your sins and the uncircumcision of your flesh, hath he quickened together with him, HAVING FORGIVEN YOU **ALL** TRESPASSES; Blotting out the handwriting of ordinances that was against us, which was contrary to us, and took it out of the way, nailing it to his cross" (Colossians 2:13,14).

"And by him all that BELIEVE are justified from **ALL** THINGS, from which ye could not be justified by the law of Moses" (Acts 13:39).

Am I not to believe the Bible when it reads "**ALL**"? If **ALL** my sins are forgiven, what sins do I have left to send me to hell? **NONE**.

Reason 5 – In the book of Hebrews, the writer tells us that those that are sanctified are "perfected forever". How does one get sanctified? We are told by Jesus himself in Acts 26:18,

"To open their eyes, and to turn them from darkness to light, and from the power of Satan unto God, that they may receive forgiveness of sins, and inheritance among them which **ARE SANCTIFIED BY FAITH** that is **IN ME."**

We clearly see that we are sanctified by **faith in Jesus**; NOT faith in ourselves, the law or works. If 100% of our faith is in Jesus, then we are perfected forever.

"For by one offering he hath **PERFECTED FOREVER** them that are sanctified" (Heb 10:14).

Since, I am perfected FOREVER, how can I lose my salvation?

Reason 6 – Salvation is a GIFT and not a reward. There a MANY verses that read salvation is a GIFT. We see this in Eph 2:8-9, Rom 6:23 and Rom 5:15-20, which reads:

But not as the offence, so also is the **FREE GIFT**. For if through the offence of one many be dead, much more the grace of God, and the **GIFT BY GRACE**, which is by one man, Jesus Christ, hath abounded unto many. And not as it was by one that sinned, so is the **GIFT**: for the judgment was by one to condemnation, but the **FREE GIFT** is of many offences unto justification. For if by one man's offence death reigned by one; much more they which receive abundance of grace and of the **GIFT OF RIGHTEOUSNESS** shall reign in life by one, Jesus Christ. Therefore as by the offence of one judgment came upon all men to condemnation; even so by the righteousness of one the

FREE GIFT came upon all men unto justification of life. For as by one man's disobedience many were made sinners, so by the obedience of one shall many be made righteous. Moreover the law entered, that the offence might abound. But where sin abounded, grace did much more abound.

Salvation is NOT a gift if one has to do something to earn it. IF one cannot earn it, how can one lose it? Also, how many times does the Bible need to tell us that salvation is **FREE** before we will actually believe it?

Reason 7 – Jesus said that nothing will be plucked out of His hand or the Father's hand.

"And I give unto them eternal life; and they shall never perish, neither shall **ANY MAN pluck** them out of my hand. My Father, which gave them me, is greater than all; and no man is able **to pluck them out** of my Father's hand" (John 10:28,29).

If one could lose their salvation, then someone or something "plucked them out of His hand". I find that to be impossible for anything to pluck us out of God's hand. The same holds true in Romans 38,39.

"For I am persuaded, that NEITHER death, nor life, nor angels, nor principalities, nor powers, nor things present, nor things to come, nor height, nor depth, nor any other creature, SHALL BE ABLE to separate us from the love of God, which is in Christ Jesus our Lord."

NOTHING—not even ourselves—will be able to pluck us out of His hand.

Reason 8 – A born again believer cannot lose their salvation because THEN we would be able to "boast".

"For by grace are ye saved through faith; and that not of yourselves: it is the gift of God: not of works, lest any man should boast" (Eph 2:8,9).

"Where is boasting then? It is **excluded**. By what law? Of works? Nay: but by the law of faith" (Romans 3:27).

Boasting simply means this, we can't go to the Father and say, "See, I deserve to be here because I am not a sinner like Hitler!" This is boasting before God. IF, I could lose my salvation, THEN I would be able to boast, "See, I didn't do that sin to lose my salvation like that guy over there!" A saved individual **CANNOT BOAST** about his or her salvation.

Reason 9 – The Bible says over and over that the believer is "declared righteous" by faith, belief, grace. There is NO verse that states once a believer is "declared righteous" they become unrighteous. JUSTIFIED means "declared righteous". The following are two examples.

"Being **JUSTIFIED FREELY** by his grace through the redemption that is in Christ Jesus" (Rom 3:24).

"Knowing that a man is NOT justified by the works of the law, but **by the faith** of Jesus Christ, even we have believed in Jesus Christ, that we might be justified **by the faith of Christ**, and NOT by the works of the law: for by the works of the law SHALL NO flesh be justified" (Gal 2:16).

Reason 10 – IF I could lose my salvation, then "the flesh" gets partial credit. The "born again" believer understands that "the flesh" cannot justify them AT ALL.

"For we are the circumcision, which worship God in the spirit, and rejoice in Christ Jesus, and have NO CONFIDENCE **in the flesh**" (Phil 3:3).

"For I know that in me (that is, **in my flesh**,) dwelleth NO GOOD thing" (Rom 7:18a).

"Are ye so FOOLISH? Having begun in the Spirit, are ye now made perfect **by the FLESH?**" (Gal 3:3).

Our flesh cannot please God at all. Are we to think that once we are sealed that we maintain our salvation through the flesh (works or works of the law that WE do)? Only "religion" would have us be so foolish (Gal 3:1-3).

Bonus reason – Here are two more verses to consider.
"...to an inheritance incorruptible, and undefiled, and that fadeth not away, **RESERVED** in heaven for you 5 Who are **KEPT** by the power of God through faith unto salvation ready to be revealed in the last time" (1 Peter 1:4-5). "Jude, the

servant of Jesus Christ, and brother of James, to them that **ARE SANCTIFIED** by God the Father, and **PRESERVED** in Jesus Christ, and called..." (Jude 1:1).

If I am kept by God and preserved by God, how can I lose my salvation? The simple answer is; I can't.

A QUESTION

The Bible is full of people who found salvation both as individuals and groups. The list includes: Saul, Cornelius, the Ethiopian, Simon the Sorcerer, the thief on the cross, the Philippian jailor, etc. Can you find **ONE** example in the Bible where someone lost his or her salvation in the New Testament? Here's a hint. You won't find one person named in the New Testament who lost his or her salvation. The Bible CANNOT contradict itself! It is God who keeps us, seals us, never losing us and not allowing anything to pluck us out of His hand. Believers ARE the body of Christ and nothing will ever separate us from the love of God. He sanctifies us by faith.

"For by one offering he hath **PERFECTED FOREVER** them that are sanctified" (Heb 10:14).

WOW! How great is this?! How great is grace! How great is God! Believe (put TOTAL confidence in) the Gospel of Jesus today. DON'T trust in yourself, religion, or works to save you. Salvation is FREE; a GIFT. Believe ONLY in Him (Jesus) and be eternally secured!

NOTE – For a more in depth study on eternal security, see a book titled *Secure Forever* by Tom Cucuzza.

Chapter 5

Hebrews 6:4-6

—✺—

"For it is impossible for those who were once enlightened, and have tasted of the heavenly gift, and were made partakers of the Holy Ghost and have tasted the good word of God, and the powers of the world to come, If they shall fall away, to renew them again unto repentance; seeing they crucify to themselves the Son of God afresh, and put him to an open shame" (Heb 6:4-6)

Hebrews 6:4-6 is one of the passages that are used by "religion" to say one can lose his or her salvation. This is a load of dung! Yes, Paul also used the word dung in the Bible. We have clearly shown that eternal security is prevalent in the scriptures (see previous chapter). We will use 2 Timothy to show that even if a believer loses his faith, he is still saved. Really? Yes, really! Then we will look at Hebrews 6:4-6. The Bible says once one believes/trusts the gospel, he or she is sealed. This is important in relating to 2 Timothy as the writer uses the word "seal" in that passage...

- Eph 1:13: "In whom ye also trusted, after that ye heard the word of truth, the gospel of your salvation:

29

in whom also after that ye believed, **ye were SEALED** with that holy Spirit of promise."

- Eph 4:30: "And grieve not the holy Spirit of God, whereby **ye ARE SEALED** unto the day of redemption."
- 2 Cor 1:21,22: "Now he which stablisheth us with you in Christ, and hath anointed us, is God;who **HATH ALSO SEALED US**, and given the earnest of the Spirit in our hearts."

Now let's go to 2 Timothy. Note: Timothy is a letter written from Paul to Timothy so the "WE" is referring to BELIEVERS.

- Verse 11 "It is a faithful saying: For if we be dead with him, we shall also live with him:"
- Verse 12 "If we suffer, we shall also reign with him: if we deny him, he also will deny us:"
- Verse 13 "If we believe not, yet he abideth faithful: he cannot deny himself."

Jesus CAN'T deny himself. We have seen that Jesus promised not to lose one and that nothing will pluck us out of His hand. Again, Jesus CAN'T deny himself. He can't make promises He doesn't intend to keep. Let us keep reading.

"And their word will eat as doth a canker: of whom is Hymenaeus and Philetus; who concerning the truth have erred, saying that the resurrection is past already; and **OVERTHROW** the **FAITH** of some" (2 Tim 2:17,18).

We see that some had their faith overthrown. This MEANS that they believed. Let's go to the next verse. The first word is **NEVERTHELESS**. This is the key. The word "nevertheless" means "in spite of". So some had their faith overthrown... **NEVERTHELESS**—or **in spite of this...**

"NEVERTHELESS the foundation of God standeth sure, having **THIS SEAL**, The Lord knoweth them that are his. And, let everyone that nameth the name of Christ depart from iniquity" (2 Tim 2:19).

Did you catch it? They were STILL SEALED despite their faith being overthrown.

NOTE: Read the next verses to explain "depart from iniquity". YES a believer should depart from iniquity. One reason is to build rewards of gold and silver and NOT wood hay and stubble, which will be burned at the Judgment Seat of Christ (1 Cor 3:10-15).

"But **WITHOUT FAITH** it is **IMPOSSIBLE** to please him: for he that cometh to God must believe that he is, and that he is a rewarder of them that diligently seek him" (Heb 11:6).

2 Timothy SUMMARY: these people whose faith had been overthrown were producing NOTHING. Their faith was gone! They had no more faith THUS it is impossible to please God (produce). Were they saved? YES – **NEVERTHELESS**, having **THIS SEAL**, the Lord knoweth them that **are HIS.** The Bible **CANNOT** contradict itself. It can't say in one place that if a person loses faith he or she is still sealed, THEN say the person lost his or her salvation in another.

So let's go back to Hebrews 6:4-6. It reads...

"For it is impossible for those who were **once enlightened**, and have **tasted** of the heavenly gift, and were made **partaker**s of the Holy Ghost and **have tasted** the good word of God, and the powers of the world to come, if they shall fall away, to renew them again unto repentance; seeing they crucify to themselves the Son of God afresh, and put him to an open shame."

The first point that needs to be made is this—this passage is talking about saved people. See the phrases used such as: tasted the heavenly gift, partakers of the Holy Ghost, tasted the word of God. These are definitely saved people. So we have saved people who, IF they were to "fall away", it is impossible to renew them **AGAIN** unto repentance. **STOP** for just a second. Where in this passage does it read that such people have lost their salvation? Where's the example of someone whose faith was overthrown (2 Tim gave an example)? **You won't find it**. Why? It is not there. People **ASSUME** they lost their salvation. All it reads is "it is impossible to renew them **AGAIN**". This is a true statement. How? It is quite simple actually. You **CAN'T** renew **AGAIN** something that **is still renewed** or, as 2 Timothy reads, "**still sealed**". Heb 6:4-6 is actually an eternal security passage. IF Jesus's sacrifice was NOT good enough the first time, He would have to come back down here and be crucified again (or afresh). This is what would put Him to an open shame. Look at these other passages in Hebrews.

"Who being the brightness of his glory, and the express image of his person, and upholding all things by the word of his power, when he had **BY HIMSELF** purged our sins, sat down on the right hand of the Majesty on high" (Heb 1:3).

"By the which will we are sanctified through the offering of the body of Jesus Christ **ONCE** for **ALL"** (Heb 12:10).

"But this man, after he had offered **ONE SACRIFICE** for sins **FOREVER**, sat down on the right hand of God" (Heb 10:12).

ONE sacrifice, **ONE** time, for **ALL** the sins of the world. Hebrews 6 doesn't seem so scary anymore, does it? Even IF your faith is overthrown you are still sealed. It is **IMPOSSIBLE** to renew you **AGAIN**. Jesus promised to never lose you and that nothing will be plucked out of His hand or the Father's hand. Again, it is impossible for a child of God to be renewed **AGAIN**. Once you are His child, **you are always His child.**

Are you his child? Have you believed the gospel?

Chapter 6

Hebrews 10:26

—∿∿∿—

"For if we sin wilfully after that we have received the knowledge of the truth, there remaineth no more sacrifice for sins..."

I obviously know that Bible verse well, being a smoker (see chapter 1), searching whole heartedly for the truth and what is really the gospel. By looking at it *alone*, it is a very condemning verse. It causes much panic. I know. It caused me to panic early in my walk. It *seems* like one can lose his or her salvation by sinning (see eternal security chapter). However, when one looks at the context of what is being said in Hebrews, it turns panic into **security.** What is the CONTEXT being discussed in this section of the bible? Hebrews is a letter written to Jewish people that had believed the gospel and were saved. The writer called them "Holy brethren" (Heb 3:1). What was happening? They were going **BACK** to the Levitical Law. This includes the **sacrificing of animals.** How does one know this?

But Christ being come an high priest of good things to come, by a greater and more perfect tabernacle, not made with hands, that is to say, not of this building; **Neither by the blood of GOATS and CALVES**, but by his own blood he entered in once into the holy place, **having obtained eternal redemption for US**. For if the blood of **BULLS and GOATS**, and the ashes of an heifer sprinkling the unclean, sanctifieth to the puri-fying of the flesh, how much more shall the blood of Christ, who **through the eternal Spirit offered HIMSELF** without spot to God, purge your conscience **from dead works** TO SERVE **the living God**? (Hebrews 9:11-13)

We get a lot from these verses of scripture. First, we don't get atonement by the shedding of blood from bulls and goats (Old Testament). Second, the writer said, "Obtaining eternal redemption for US". This means he was writing to saved people. Third, we see that "dead works" don't save (also see Heb 6). We are not saved by works (Rom 11:6). So **QUIT** trying to earn salvation by working; they are **DEAD** works! We are saved by the precious blood of Jesus Christ shed at the cross (1 Cor 15:1-4). However, we do works "TO SERVE" the living God. Salvation is **FREE** without works (Eph 2:8,9). We serve the Lord because we are **ALREADY** saved. Salvation and service, always keep them the separate. Hebrews 9 and 10, within the context of the book, we see that these SAVED Jewish brethren were being convinced to go BACK under the Levitical law and the animal, sacrificial system of the Old Testament. The writer is trying to convince them that JESUS was the eternal sacrifice for sin. Go back to Hebrews 1:3.

"Who being the brightness of his glory, and the express image of his person, and upholding all things by the word of his power, when he had **BY HIMSELF** purged our sins, sat down on the right hand of the Majesty on high."

This is the theme of the book of Hebrews and the issue the writer was attempting to address. Let's keep going in chapter 9. Later in the chapter, it speaks of Jesus being the sacrifice ONCE FOR ALL. In the Old Testament, the priest entered into the temple every year, but no more. For Jesus has entered into the Holy place to put away sin... AMEN.

For Christ is not entered into the holy places made with hands, which are the figures of the true; but into heaven itself, now to appear in the presence of God FOR US, **nor** yet that he should offer **HIMSELF** often, as the high priest entereth into the holy place every year with blood of others; For then must he often have suffered since the foundation of the world: but **NOW once** in the end of the world hath he appeared **to put away sin** by the sacrifice of **HIMSELF**. And as it is appointed unto men once to die, but after this the judgment: So Christ was **ONCE** offered to bear the sins of many; and unto them that look for him shall he appear the second time without sin unto salvation. (Heb 9:24-28)

In Hebrews 10, you get the same theme.

But in those sacrifices there is a remembrance again made of sins every year. For it is **not possible** that the blood of bulls and of goats should take away sins. Above when he said, Sacrifice and offering and burnt offerings and offering for sin thou wouldest not, neither hadst pleasure therein; which are offered by the law; Then said he, Lo, I come to do thy will, O God. He taketh away the first, that he may establish the second. By the which will we are sanctified through the offering of the body of Jesus Christ **ONCE** for **ALL**. But this man, after he had offered **one sacrifice** for sins **FOREVER**, sat down on the right hand of God. For by **ONE** offering he hath perfected **FOREVER** them that are sanctified. (Hebrews 10:3,4,8-10, 12, 14)

Isn't this one of the most uplifting books in the Bible? I mean, look how many times does it tells us that JESUS was the sacrifice of God, the Lamb of God that taketh away the sins of the world. How many times do we see ONCE for ALL? How about verse 14 "perfected forever"? YES, I know the other versions read "being sanctified". I am KJV1611 PREFERRED for many reasons; it reads "**are sanctified**". As if this wasn't enough, the writer, talking to saved people who were leaving Jesus and grace, wants to give assurance to these believers. It does this by saying "for he is faithful that promised". Salvation IS about Jesus's promise to us!

Let us draw near with a true heart in FULL assurance of faith, having our hearts sprinkled from an evil conscience, and our bodies washed with pure water. Let us hold fast the profession of our faith without wavering; (**FOR HE IS FAITHFUL THAT PROMISED**) And let us consider one another to provoke unto love and to good works. (Heb 10:22-24)

HERE IS THE VERSE: "For if we sin wilfully after that we have received the knowledge of the truth, there remaineth no more sacrifice for sins." When you read 1 John 3:9 (later in the book; Chapter 13), you will see that we are all practicing sinners. Many of the sins Christians commit are willful. Let us now review Romans 7:14-25 to see Paul's current battle with sin. What I mean by "current" is this—when he wrote Romans, he was currently sinning. Look at the verbs. They are all present tense.

> For we know that the law is spiritually; but **I am** carnal, sold under sin. For that which **I do** I allow not: for what I would, that do I not; but what I hate, that **do I**. If then **I do** that which I would not, I consent unto the law that it is good. Now then it is no more I that do it, but sin that dwelleth in me. For I know that in me (that is, in my flesh,) dwelleth no good thing: for to will is present with me; but how to perform that which is good **I find not.** For the good that I would **I do not**: but the evil which I would not, that **I DO**. Now if I do that I would not, it is no more I that do it, but sin that dwelleth in me. I find then a law, that, when I would do good, evil is present with me. For I delight in the law of God after the inward man: But I see another law in my members, warring against the law of my mind, and bringing me into captivity to the law of sin which is in my members.

O wretched man that I am! who shall deliver me from the body of this death? I thank God through Jesus Christ our Lord. So then with the mind I myself serve the law of God; but with the flesh the law of sin. (Romans 7:14-25)

The Greek word for DO in verse 19 is *prassw*. It means "to practice, to habitually commit". YES, Paul practiced sin. Sin is sin; whether willful or not. Most sin is willful. What was the willful sin going on here? It was rejecting Jesus's sacrifice and sacrificing animals in His place. Either way, if we sin after we hear the knowledge of truth, whether willfully or not, there **REMAINS NO SACRIFICE FOR SINS.** What a TRUE STATEMENT this is. Today, there is **NO** goat, **NO** lamb, **NO** animal sacrifice that **REMAINS** that can take away sin. Today, there **REMAINS** no more sacrifice for sin. WHY? The **ONCE** for **ALL** sacrifice happened 2,000 years ago by Jesus. This is the **CONTEXT** of the book! We must look at who the book is written to, what is going on, and the solution. The purpose was convincing **saved people** who had gone **BACK** to sacrificing animals that no more animal sacrifices are needed. **QUIT** doing it! There **REMAINS** no sacrifice for sin. Their actions were pretty much saying, "Jesus's sacrifice was NOT good enough." This belief trods under foot the Son of God (verse 29).

PERSONAL QUESTION: How many professing Christians do you know who say, "Jesus's sacrifice was not good enough" by adding to the gospel?

Many religious people use this passage to say a person can lose his or her salvation. Hog wash! In verse 14 it reads "perfected forever". If a born again believer is perfected for-ever, how can he or she lose that salvation?! The religious will always take scripture out of context! Again, He was telling these Jewish brethren who were sacrificing animals, "There remains no sacrifice for sins!" If we continue reading in Hebrews we read that these people believed the gospel and did some things for the kingdom (verses 32-35). Verse 35 is another assurance of salvation verse.

> "Cast not away therefore your confidence, which hath great recompence of **REWARD**." Then verse 36 continues, "For ye have need of patience, that, after ye have done the will of God, ye might receive the promise."

> What is the will of God?

> "...and this is the WILL OF HIM that sent me, that every one which seeth the Son, and believeth on him, may have everlasting life: and I will raise him up at the last day (John 6:40).

What are the promises of God? Salvation is promised to those who believe on the completed work of Jesus at the cross (that's FREE a GIFT of God; Eph 2:8,9). REWARDS are promised to those who abide in the faith and bear fruit worthy of repentance (change of mind).

Have you believed (trusted) in the **ONCE FOR ALL** sacrifice of Jesus or do you believe (trusting) in something else? Maybe you are trusting in what Hebrews calls "**dead works**". If you have trusted in this sacrifice of Jesus alone, you are **perfected forever** (Heb 10:14)

Chapter 7

Can I be cast away?

———❦———

"**B**ut I keep under my body, and bring it into subjection: lest that by any means, when I have preached to others, I myself should be a cast away" (1 Cor 9:27).

The religious like to use this verse to say one can lose his or her salvation. "You must keep your body under subjection or you will be castaway from heaven," is proclaimed from many pulpits. This is simply another false interpretation of scripture. We have seen the Bible tell us that salvation is FREE (Rom 5:15-20), that he who comes to Jesus will in no wise be cast out (John 6:37). Why would Paul be worried about being cast out of heaven when he told us ALL the believer's sins were forgiven (Col 3:13,14) and all believers are sealed unto the day of redemption (Eph 4:30)? What is really being said in this passage? Like many scriptures, we need to look at the context (verses before and after). Go back to 1 Cor 9:24. It reads,

"Know ye not that they which run in a race run all, but one receiveth a prize? So run that ye may obtain."

Notice the word "prize". Salvation is **not** a prize; it is a gift (Rom 6:23). As a result, Paul is talking about something else here. What is Paul trying to obtain? We find out in the very next verse.

"And every man that striveth for the mastery is temperate in all things. Now they do it **to obtain** a corruptible **crown**, but we an **incorruptible**" (1 Cor 9:25).

We see that Paul was concerned with being cast away from earning an **incorruptible crown**. As an illustration of this, we can use the example of any sporting event. I will choose the Olympics. Let's just say there are 100 Olympians that qualified for the 100-meter dash. After a few rounds, only eight have made it to the finals. This means that ninety-two Olympians have been *"castaway"* from earning a medal. After the eight man final, five more are *"cast away"* from earning a medal. By earning a silver and bronze medal, two more are *"cast away"* from earning the gold medal. In the past, the winner would have received a crown called an "olive wreath crown". This was the coveted prize. However, these crowns were corruptible and over time, would fade away. The crown Paul was striving to earn was an incorruptible crown given by the Lord in eternity.

This is the same thing within Christianity. Like the Olympians, the believer is running a race to earn a crown. The Olympians were cast away from earning a prize, BUT were still Olympic athletes and competed at the events. The same applies to all sealed believers. All born again believers will be allowed to compete for a prize. If they don't win this prize (there are other prizes), they are still born again and going to heaven; NOTHING can change that. Paul wanted to keep his body under subjection to earn (win) a crown. Salvation from hell is FREE. Rewards are earned or obtained by effort. Rewards include crowns. I believe there are 3-5 different crowns that can be earned. Since this book is about salvation from hell and explaining scripture used to deny salvation by faith in the gospel alone, I will not delve into the "rewards" doctrine of scripture. However, it is clear that salvation in 1 Cor 9:27 is not in view when looking at the context of the passage. If you have believed the gospel, that Jesus *died for your sins* and rose again, you will never be cast away from heaven.

Chapter 8

Faith without works - James 2

—⌒∾⌒—

Often when discussing the Bible with the "religious" about salvation, you will hear, "But faith without works is dead"! "What about James 2"? Does James 2 tell us that works are needed for salvation? No, James is simply a book written to "already saved" people exhorting them to do good works. In this chapter we will examine James 2 and the statement: "Faith without works is dead." First, we need some verses that say we are saved without works.

- "For by grace are ye SAVED through faith; and that not of yourselves: it is the gift of God: **NOT OF WORKS**, lest any man should boast" (Eph 2:8,9).
- "Where is boasting then? It is excluded. By what law? of **WORKS**? **NAY:** but by the law of faith" (Rom 3:27).
- "But to him that **WORKETH NOT**, but believeth on him that justifieth the ungodly, his faith is counted for righteousness" (Rom 4:5).
- "Even as David also describeth the blessedness of the man, unto whom God imputeth righteousness **WITHOUT WORKS**" (Rom 4:6).

- "**NOT BY WORKS** of righteousness which we have done, but according to his mercy He saved us, by the washing of regeneration, and renewing of the Holy Ghost" (Titus 3:5).
- "And if by grace, then is it **NO MORE OF WORKS**: otherwise grace is **NO MORE** grace. But if it be of works, then it is **NO MORE** grace: otherwise work is no more work" (Rom 11:6).

I think you get the point. We are not saved by works. It is clear. Then what about, "Faith without works is dead"? This is a true statement. *However, "dead" does not mean "unsaved".* It means "inactive/useless". Let us start with verse 14.

"What doth it profit, my brethren, though a man say he hath faith, and have not works? Can faith save him?" (James 2:14).

The first part of this verse uses the word "profit". We have already seen that salvation is a gift (Rom 5:15-20) and not of works. As a result, you cannot "profit" salvation. In the second part of the verse, James asks his saved brethren, "Can faith save him"? Well, the answer is no. Stay with me! The question we need to ask is, "Save them from what?" *It is **not** from hell, as James is writing to believers*—they are already saved (use of bretheren in James 1:2). Hell is not mentioned one time in James. What are they being saved from? Judgment (see verse 13). Faith will not save a believer from judgment. There are two other forms of judgment mentioned in the Bible.

- The chastening hand of God. God will discipline His own. (Heb 12:5,6)
- The **Judgment** Seat of Christ where our **works** are tested. (1 Cor 3:10-15)

Let's go to verse 18. Before I start, we have to realize who is speaking. **IT IS NOT JAMES**. Seriously! James has created a fictional character that begins to speak... sort of like me telling you a joke: "one guy said to the other"; I have just created two fictitious men. How do we know this? Verse 18 starts with, "yea **a MA**N may say". James didn't say, "Verily I tell you" or "I say unto thee". James creates a fictional man (yea **a MAN** may say). It is **this man** that is now talking. James actually calls the man **vain** in verse 20. I will substitute Bob for "man" to show clarity.

> Yea, **Bob** (a man) may say, "Thou hast faith, and I have works: shew me thy faith without thy works, and I will shew thee my faith by my works." Thou believest that there is one God; thou doest well: the devils also believe, and tremble but wilt thou know, O vain **Bob** (man), that faith without works is dead? (Taken from James 2:18-20)

Yes, it is HUMAN VAINITY that thinks we have anything to offer God for salvation. The Bible is clear. Salvation is a FREE GIFT to anyone who believes the simple gospel message.

> Was not Abraham our father justified by works, when he had offered Isaac his son upon the altar (verse 21)?

The same question we asked about the word "save" in verse 14 is the same question we need to ask in verse 18. The question is, "Justified before whom?" It is **NOT** God.

"What shall we say then that Abraham our father, as pertaining to the flesh, hath found? For if Abraham were justified by works, he hath whereof to glory; but **NOT** before God" (Rom 4:1,2).

WORKS justify us before **Man**. Man looketh on the outward but God knoweth the heart (1 Sam 16:7). On to verse 22, which reads:

"Seest thou how faith wrought with his works, and by works was faith made **perfect.**"

Remember Jesus's ministry. He said to his disciples many times "ye of LITTLE faith", while telling the Gentile centurion "I have seen no GREATER faith than this"? From this we know that there are different levels of faith. WORKS bring faith to perfection. Notice the word, "**perfect**". We see this word "perfect" when talking about works in 2 Tim 3:16,17.

"All scripture is given by inspiration of God, and is profitable for doctrine, for reproof, for correction, for instruction in righteousness: That the **man of God** may be **perfect**, thoroughly furnished unto all good works."

NOTICE, "the man of God" (*already saved*) may be **perfect** unto all good works. This is **not** saying that any flesh can be perfect. It is saying we are to be prepared **unto** all good works. This is confirmed in Titus.

> "This is a faithful saying, and these things I will that thou affirm constantly, that they which have believed in God **might** be careful to maintain **good works**. These things are good and **profitable** unto men" (Titus 3:8).

I hope this helped explain "faith without works is dead". It is a true statement. Faith that does not work is "useless or inactive". It doesn't **profit** anything. It is **not** saying that works are necessary FOR salvation as that would contradict so many passages of scripture. FAITH ALONE in the gospel of Jesus saves from hell, but without works, that "saving faith" is unprofitable; it is "useless". It will not produce anything. James is a book written to exhort people who are already saved to do good works.

Chapter 9

Even the devils believe and tremble

"Thou believest that there is one God; thou doest well:
the devils also believe, and tremble" (James 2:19).

A s soon as one quotes John 3:16 and John 6:47, the
works for salvation-ist will immediately quote James
2:19 in an attempt to say that belief in Jesus is not sufficient. They will respond with, "Believing is not enough, for
even the devils believe and tremble". This chapter will equip
any born again believer with the ammo they need to rebuke
such a statement. The first part will be a bit repetitive as
reason number one was already stated in James 2. However,
I wanted to look at this particular phrase with a magnifying
glass. James 2:18-20 reads,

"Yea, **a man** may say, Thou hast faith, and I have
works: shew me thy faith without thy works, and I
will shew thee my faith by my works. Thou believest
that there is one God; thou doest well: the devils also

believe, and tremble. But wilt thou know, **O vain man**, that faith without works is dead?"

Again, the first explanation was already stated in a previous chapter. James is not talking. James creates a fictitious character. He does this by saying "yea a man may say". It is this man that begins to speak. James responds to "this man" in verse 20 calling "this man" vain.

To see it more clearly, substitute a name (Bob) for the word "man" in both verses (18 and 20). It will become much clearer. It is so true. It is complete human vain-ity that a man thinks he can offer anything to God for salvation; for our works are as filthy rags unto the Lord (this found in Isaiah). How can we "earn" grace? How can we "earn" something that by definition is "unmerited favor" (grace)? The answer is obvious, **we can't**.

The second thing I would like you to notice about this passage is in verse 19: "thou believest there is **one** God". Well, many people believe there is **one** God. Muslims believe there is one God. Jews believe there is one God. Jehovah's Witnesses believe there is one God. The Pharisees believed there was one God. I think you get the point. Believing there is **one** God does not save. Belief that Jesus, God in the flesh, died for ALL your sins does save.

The third point is the term "kinsman redeemer". It is an Old Testament term that tells us that one can pay a debt for a relative who was in trouble. The book of Ruth is an earthly example of how this works. Jesus came to be our kinsman redeemer. He did this to pay our sin debt when we are not capable of paying it ourselves. How did He do this? Jesus humbled himself and became a man to redeem us from the curse of the law. Since we are created beings from Adam, we are all related. Only Adam and Eve were created directly from God. As a result of this, we are all born with a sin nature. In Romans 5:14-20 where salvation is stated as being a **FREE GIFT**, we see that we have received another gift. We received the gift of a sin nature from Adam.

Nevertheless death reigned from Adam to Moses, even over them that had not sinned after the similitude of **Adam's transgression**, who is the figure of him that was to come but not as the offence, so also is the free gift. For if through **the offence of one many be dead**, much more the grace of God, and the gift by grace, which is by one man, Jesus Christ, hath abounded unto many. And not as it was by one that sinned, so is the gift: for the **judgment was by one to condemnation**, but the free gift is of many offences unto justification. For if **by one man's offence** death reigned by one; much more they which receive abundance of grace and of the gift of righteousness shall reign in life by one, Jesus Christ. Therefore as **by the offence of one** judgment came upon all men to condemnation; even so by the righteousness of one the free gift came upon all men unto justification of life. For as **by one man's disobedience** many were made sinners, so by the obedience of one shall many be made righteous. Moreover the law entered, that the offence might abound. But where sin abounded, grace did much more abound.

The one man here is Adam (Rom 5:14). Because of this gift from Adam, all men are condemned (not all gifts are good). What does this have to do with Jesus being our kinsman redeemer and James 2? Simple: devils were also created directly from God. There is no evidence that devils can pro-create with other devils. As a result, Jesus cannot become the "kinsman redeemer" for devils. Jesus would then have to take the form of each devil and die a separate death to vindicate them. The devils believe that Jesus exists, but cant "trust in Him" for salvation.

The final point was already mentioned. Devils were created without a sin nature—thus, they chose to sin. Man, with the exception of Adam and Eve, were not created this way. We are all born sinners. Thus God chose to die for the sins of mankind. That's why salvation is truly free. Because the sin nature was also free. This should be enough to refute anyone that uses **this passage** to say belief is not enough. However, I got some more. Yep. If one still can't see that belief is enough, I suggest using these scriptures.

- JESUS SAID—That whosoever BELIEVETH in him should not perish, but HAVE eternal life (John 3:15)
- JESUS SAID—For God so loved the world, that he gave his only begotten Son, that whosoever BELIEVETH in him should not perish, but HAVE everlasting life (John 3:16)
- JESUS SAID—He that BELIEVETH on him is NOT condemned: but he that believeth not is condemned already, because he hath not believed in the name of the only begotten Son of God (John 3:18)
- JESUS SAID—Verily, verily, I say unto you, He that heareth my word, and BELIEVETH on him that sent

me, HATH everlasting life, and shall not come into condemnation; but is passed from death unto life. (John 5:24)

- JESUS SAID—Jesus answered and said unto them, this is the work of God, that ye BELIEVE on him whom he hath sent. (John 6:29)
- JESUS SAID—And Jesus said unto them, I am the bread of life: he that cometh to me shall never hunger; and he that BELIEVETH on me shall NEVER thirst (John 6:35)
- JESUS SAID—And this is the will of him that sent me, that every one which seeth the Son, and BELIEVETH on him, may HAVE everlasting life: and I will raise him up at the last day (John 6:40)
- JESUS SAID—Verily, verily, I say unto you, He that BELIEVETH on me HATH everlasting life (John 6:47)
- JESUS SAID—He that BELIEVETH on me, as the scripture hath said, out of his belly shall flow rivers of LIVING water. (John 7:38)
- JESUS SAID—Jesus said unto her, I am the resurrection, and the life: he that BELIEVETH in me, though he were dead, yet shall he LIVE: (John 11:25)

I think you get the point. Jesus cannot contradict himself. He who believes (trusts) in Jesus (not themselves) will have everlasting life. I would like anyone who believes works are a requirement for salvation to answer this question from Jesus "internally". Jesus asked this question. I would like you to pretend that He is asking **you** this question.

JESUS SAID, "And whosoever liveth and believeth in me shall never die. Believest thou this?" (John 11:26).

If the works for salvation-ist were honest, he would have replied, "**No Lord**, I **don't** believe you; for even the devils believe and tremble"!

With all due respect, after reading all the Jesus said's above, doesn't that sound like a very foolish answer? Anyone who uses that phrase to say belief is not enough to save is gravely mistaken. They need help. Religion has gotten to them. If you have used this term in the same matter, stop it! Religion says "do" for salvation, but Jesus says "done". "And brought them out, and said, 'Sirs, what must I do to be saved?' And they said, '**Believe on the Lord Jesus Christ**, and thou shalt be saved, and thy house'" (Acts 16:30-31).

Chapter 10

Repent of your sins?

———∞∞∞———

To go to heaven, you MUST repent of your sins. Wrong! How many protestants believe one **MUST** "repent of their sins" (or turn from their sins) to go to heaven? If I had to guesstimate, I would say 80%. This teaching is what Galatians calls "another gospel", a perverted gospel that frustrates grace. It does **not** save. Why do so many people believe this term? It is the direct result of what is being taught in the pulpits today. Who teaches this? Just about every *"famous"* protestant evangelical today preaches this heresy. I did not name names, as I would feel the need to provide references. Pick a famous protestant evangelical and search to see if they use this phrase *FOR* salvation. You will find it easily. This will be one of the longest chapters since this phrase "repent of your sins" is sending more people to hell than anything else today. We will spend a lot of time in Galatians. Then we will visit Acts and Romans to conclude. **FIRST AND MOST IMPORTANT**: We need to **DEFINE** sin. The definition of sin is in 1 John.

"Whosoever committeth sin transgresseth also the law: for sin is the transgression of the law" (1 John 3:4).

We see from this passage that sin IS "transgression of the LAW". For example, if I stole something that was not mine, then I have transgressed the law, "thou shalt not steal". Thus, I have sinned. However, if a person says that one must turn from his or her sins FOR salvation, *that is the same thing as saying one must keep the law or keep the law better.* WHY?

Sin IS transgression of the LAW.

turn from sin = keep the law (or keep the law better).

Do you see it? **IF YOU DID NOT GRASP THIS; PLEASE RE-READ IT AGAIN** (and again, and again) Do **NOT** continue from here **UNTIL** this concept is understood. Once you have grasped this, we will move on to Galatians.

I marvel that ye are so soon removed from him that called you into the grace of Christ unto **ANOTHER GOSPEL**: Which is not another; but there be some that trouble you, and would **PERVERT THE GOSPEL** of Christ. But though we, or an angel from heaven, preach any other gospel unto you than that which we have preached unto you, let him be accursed. (Galatians 1:6-8)

We see that someone had come into Galatia and preached "another/perverted" gospel. What was being preached to them? **AFTER** Paul goes through his conversion and his dispute with Peter, he gets into the problem.

"Knowing that a man is **NOT** justified by the works of the law, but **by the faith of Jesus Christ**, even we have believed in Jesus Christ, that we might be justified **by the faith of Christ**, and **NOT** by the works of the law: **for by the works of the law shall NO FLESH BE JUSTIFIED**" (Gal 2:16).

"I do not **FRUSTRATE** the grace of God: for if righteousness comes by the law, then Christ is dead in vain" (Gal 2:21).

Frustrate does not mean to irritate in this passage; it means "to make void; to nullify". **The LAW nullifies GRACE.** "I do not "make void/nullify" (frustrate) the grace of God, for if righteousness comes by the law, Christ died in vain." This simply means, if the law could save you, Christ would not have had to die. Let's keep going in Galatians.

O **foolish** Galatians, who hath bewitched you, that ye should not obey the truth, before whose eyes Jesus Christ hath been evidently set forth, crucified among you? This only would I learn of you, Received ye the Spirit by the works of the law, or by the hearing of faith? Are ye so foolish? having begun in the Spirit, are ye now made perfect by the flesh? (Gal 3:1-3)

Paul is asking them, "Did your salvation (sealed by the Holy Spirit) come from the LAW of the hearing of faith?" The answer should be obvious (Eph 1:13,14; Rom 10:17). Someone has bewitched them telling them that the law needed to be kept. He called them "**foolish**" for thinking they are made perfect by the flesh. In Philippians 3:3 we read,

"For we are the circumcision, which worship God in the SPIRIT, and rejoice in Christ Jesus, and have **NO CONFIDENCE in the FLESH.**"

Back to Galatians.

Even as Abraham believed God, and it was accounted to him for righteousness. Know ye therefore that they which are of FAITH, the same are the children of Abraham. For as many as are of the works of the law **ARE UNDER THE CURSE**: for it is written, Cursed is every one that continueth **not in ALL things** which are written in the book of the law to do them. But that **NO MAN** is justified by the law in the sight of God, it is evident: for the just shall live by faith. Christ hath redeemed us from the curse of the law, being made a curse for us: for it is written, Cursed is every one that hangeth on a tree: That the blessing of Abraham might come on the Gentiles through Jesus Christ; that we might **RECEIVE THE PROMISE** of the Spirit through **FAITH**. And this I say, that the covenant, that was confirmed before of God in Christ, the law, which was four hundred and thirty years after, cannot disannul, that it should make **the promise of NONE EFFECT**. For if the inheritance be of the law, **it is NO MORE of promise**: but God gave it to Abraham **BY PROMISE. (**Gal 3:6,7,10-12,14,17,18)

Salvation is about God's **PROMISE** to us and **NOT** how well we keep the LAW. This **PROMISE** comes by faith only. **The LAW** makes **VOID** the promise.

"For the **promise**, that he should be the heir of the world, was **not to Abraham**, or to his seed, **through the law**, but through the righteousness of faith. For **if they** which are of the law be heirs, **faith IS MADE VOID**, and **the promise** made of **NONE EFFECT**" (Romans 4:13,14).

Is the law then against the promises of God? God forbid: for if there had been a law given which could have given life, verily righteousness should have been by the law. But the scripture hath concluded all under sin, that the **PROMISE BY FAITH** of Jesus Christ might be given to them that **BELIEVE**. But before faith came, we were kept under the law, shut up unto the faith which should afterwards be revealed. Wherefore the LAW was our SCHOOLMASTER to bring us unto Christ, that we might be justified by faith. But after that faith is come, we **ARE NO LONGER** under a schoolmaster (LAW). For ye are all the children of God **by faith in Christ Jesus**. (Gal 3:21-26; commentary added)

Tell me, ye that desire to be under the law, do ye not hear the law? For it is written, that Abraham had two sons, the one by a bondmaid, the other by a **free**woman. But he who was of the bondwoman was born after the flesh; but he of the **free**woman was by

promise. So then, brethren, we are not children of the bondwoman, but of the **FREE.** (Gal 4:21-23, 31)

As you can clearly see, a born again believer IS no longer under the schoolmaster (the LAW) but under GRACE. A believer is of the FREE woman by promise.

SUMMARY OF GALATIANS

Sin is defined as transgression of the law. When one states that one MUST repent of his or her sins FOR salvation, he is putting that person "under the law" (schoolmaster). WHY? "Turn from sin" = "keep the law", because sin is transgression of the law. Salvation is by **PROMISE** through **FAITH** in the gospel of Jesus alone. The **LAW** makes faith **VOID** and the PROMISE of none effect (Rom 3:13,14). Does anyone want to make faith void? Does anyone want to make God's promise of none effect? No? Then **STOP** preaching this "turn from your sins" **FOR** salvation message! Today's major protestant evangelicals **are preaching "another/perverted gospel"** (1:6-8).

Stand fast therefore in the liberty wherewith Christ hath made us **free**, and be not entangled again with the yoke of bondage. Behold, I Paul say unto you, that if ye be circumcised, Christ shall profit you nothing. For I testify again to every man that is circumcised, that he is a debtor to do the **WHOLE LAW**. Christ is become of NO EFFECT unto you, whosoever of you are justified by the law; ye are fallen from grace. (Gal 5:1-4)

NOTICE – it does not read "fallen from salvation". You cannot lose your salvation (see chapter on eternal security). Paul then writes what he wanted to happened to those who preached the law for salvation. "I would they were even CUT OFF which trouble you" (Gal 5:12). I also found it funny in Galatians 6:13 when Paul wrote this:

"For **neither they themselves** who are circumcised **keep the law**; but desire to have you circumcised, that they may glory in your flesh."

This verse simply means the people who were preaching law really couldn't keep it! Remember, if one is required to keep one law for salvation, then that person is a endebted to the whole law (Gal 5:3). Who can keep the whole law? **Nobody!** This is why Christ had to die! Now let us look into the book of Acts to see what was written about the law and salvation. I will set this up a bit. We will clearly see that the Law of Moses is not needed for salvation. In fact, the disciples gave "no such commandment" to keep the law to be saved. We'll start with the first verses of Acts 15.

And certain men which came down from Judaea taught the brethren, and said, Except ye be circumcised after the manner of Moses, ye cannot be saved. When therefore Paul and Barnabas **had no small dissension** and disputation with them, they determined that Paul and Barnabas, and certain other of them, should go up to Jerusalem unto the apostles and elders about this question. (Acts 15:1,2)

We read that certain people believed that one must be circumcised to be saved. They made this a "requirement" for salvation. We see in verse 2 that this was "no small dissension". In other words, it was a big dispute/debate. Let's resume in verse 5.

> "...but there rose up certain of the sect of the Pharisees which believed, saying, That it was needful to circumcise them, **AND to command them to keep the law of Moses**. And the apostles and elders came together for to consider of this matter" (Acts 15:5,6).

From these verses, we see that circumcision was **not the only thing** that needed to be done. The message was that one needed to keep the Law of Moses. I believe there are 613 Old Testament laws, but most are familiar with ten that Moses delivered from the mount. Peter was compelled to speak.

> And when there had been much disputing, Peter rose up, and said unto them, "Men and brethren, ye know how that a good while ago God made choice among us, that the Gentiles by my mouth should hear the word of the **GOSPEL**, and **BELIEVE.** And God, which knoweth the hearts, bare them witness, giving them the Holy Ghost, even as he did unto us; And put no difference between us and them, purifying their hearts **BY FAITH.** Now therefore why **tempt ye God**, to put a yoke upon the neck of the disciples, which neither our fathers nor we were able to bear? But

we **believe** that **through the grace** of the LORD Jesus Christ we shall be saved, even as they." (Acts 15:7-11)

Much was said in these five verses. We have learned that one needs to hear the word of the gospel (1 Cor 15:1-4) and believe. We also learned that there is no difference between Jews and Gentiles (us and them). We **CLEARLY** see that **adding the law** to the gospel **"tempts God"** by putting a yoke around people's necks. We also are told that "the fathers" could not bear that yoke. In other words, they couldn't keep the law, either (does this remind you of the Galatians 6:13 passage?). Verse 11 tells us that **we are saved by GRACE**, after talking about how the Gentiles were being accepted by God. He concludes in verse 23 and 24.

And they wrote letters by them after this manner; "The apostles and elders and brethren send greeting unto the brethren which are of the Gentiles in Antioch and Syria and Cilicia. Forasmuch as we have heard, that certain which went out from us have troubled you with words, subverting your souls, saying, Ye must be circumcised, **AND** keep the law: to whom we gave **NO SUCH COMMANDMENT."** (Acts 15:23,24)

The apostles gave **"no such commandment"** to keep the law to "be saved". *If the apostles gave no such commandment, why are so many Protestants telling people you must "turn from your sins" (keep the law) to go to heaven?* "But we believe that through the grace of the LORD Jesus Christ we shall be saved, even as they" (Acts 15:11).

Now let's take a look at a few verses from Romans. I won't go into detail explaining these verses. They are pretty clear. It does, however, give even more support to "no law" TO be saved.

Being justified **FREELY** by his **GRACE** through the redemption that is in Christ Jesus: Whom God hath set forth to be a propitiation through faith in his blood, to declare his righteousness for the remission of sins that are past, through the forbearance of God; To declare, I say, at this time his righteousness: that he might be just, and the justifier of him which believeth in Jesus. Where is boasting then? It is excluded. By what law? of works? Nay: but **by the law of faith**. Therefore we **CONCLUDE** that a man is justified **by faith WITHOUT** the deeds of THE LAW. (Romans 3:24-28)

Romans 3:24-28 is pretty clear. In fact I am not sure you get much clearer than that. There is another CLEAR passage in Romans about the law. Before we get to the second Romans passage, let's check out Philippians 3:9, which will define the term "our own righteousness".

"And be found in him, not having mine **own righteousness, which is of the law**, but that which is through the faith of Christ, the righteousness, which is of God by faith"

Now back to Romans.

"For , being ignorant of God's righteousness, and going about to establish their **own righteousness**, have **NOT** submitted themselves unto the righteousness of God. For Christ **is the end of the law** FOR righteousness to everyone that **believeth"** (Romans 10:3,4).

Why do so many Protestant professing believers add "repent of sins" to the gospel and create what Galatians calls "another gospel"? **Why** do so many continue to add the law to salvation? **Why** do so many add their **own righteousness**, which is of the law (Phil 3:9)? How many times does the Bible need to tell us, "no law for salvation"? Remember Romans 4:13,14:

"For the promise, that he should be the heir of the world, was **NOT** to Abraham, or to his seed, **through the law**, but through the righteousness of faith. For if they which are of the law be heirs, **faith is made void**, and **the promise made of none effect."**

Chapter 11

Meaning of the word "repent"

—◦◦◦—

We have seen that "repent of your sins" is actually another gospel that does NOT save. It puts a person under the law, the whole law. What does the Bible mean when it says to "repent"? Here are a few points and passages that will help explain the true definition of the word "repent".

- POINT 1: in the KJV1611 the phrase of "repent of your sins" is NOT in the Bible anywhere. The word "repent" IS in the Bible, but NOT "repent of sins". Someone ADDED the "of sins" phrase.

- POINT 2: In the Old Testament, God repented several times. Did God "turn from His sins"? Jonah 3:10 says, "And God saw their works, that they turned from their evil way; and GOD REPENTED of the evil, that he had said that he would do unto them; and he did it not."

- POINT 3: Repent in the Greek is *metanoia*, it means to "think differently; to change your mind". God simply "changed His mind".

- POINT 4: one does need to REPENT. One MUST change his or her mind FROM anything he or she THINKS is going to save him or her TO the gospel.
- POINT 5: LET'S take a look at three passages of scripture the "religious" use to say one MUST repent of his or her sins. They are in Matthew, Luke and Acts.

"In those days came John the Baptist, preaching in the wilderness of Judaea, saying, REPENT YE: for the kingdom of heaven is at hand" (Matt 3:1,2).

The religious will say, "SEE, you must turn from your sins (REPENT)". Remember, it does not read "of sins". The answer to this passage is Matthew 3:9, which reads,

"And **THINK NOT** to say within yourselves, 'We have Abraham to our father': for I say unto you, that God is able of these stones to raise up children unto Abraham."

Do you see it? These people were **THINKING** that just because they had Abraham as the father (Jewish), they were "automatically" saved. They were **THINKING the WRONG** thing. They needed to "change their minds; think differently"! They needed to "repent".

Jesus said, "I tell you, nay: but, except ye repent, ye shall all likewise perish" (Luke 13:3).

The religious would say, "SEE, you must repent (turn from your sins)." What does the Bible say? Go back and read the verse that comes before, then the verse that comes after it. You will SEE the problem.

"And Jesus answering said unto them, **SUPPOSE YE** that these Galilaeans were sinners above all the Galilaeans, because they suffered such things?" (Luke 13:2).

"Or those eighteen, upon whom the tower in Siloam fell, and slew them, **THINK YE** that they were sinners above all men that dwelt in Jerusalem?" (Luke 13:4)

We **CLEARLY** see that they were **THINKING** (suppose ye) they were righteous because they were NOT sinners like the ones whom were killed. They needed to **SUPPOSE OR THINK** something different. They needed to "change their minds" (repent). I believe most professing Christians fall into this category. Because they have turned from many sins, they **THINK** they "are not sinners like most". These folks need to repent (change their minds) and believe the gospel or they, too will perish.

We also have the word "repent" in Acts many times. One such instance is in Acts 3:19 which reads,

"Repent therefore and be converted, that your sins maybe blotted out."

Now go back a few verses and read 13-18.

There, Peter is telling Jewish people that they crucified their promised Messiah. Verse 14 reads that they denied Him. Peter was simply telling them to **change their minds** about who Jesus really was and to be converted so their sins would be blotted out—change your mind and be converted.

We see, through analyzing scripture, "repent" simply means "to change your mind, to think differently". When Jesus said, "Repent and believe the gospel", He was telling them to "change their minds" and believe the gospel. Did they change their minds? Some did, but for the most part, the answer is "no". How do we know? They crucified Him. PERSONALLY, if I hear one more preacher tell people they must "repent of their sins" to go to heaven, I think I am going to bang my head up against the wall! THEN I'll bandage myself up and continue proclaiming the **REAL** gospel.

Chapter 12

I never knew you

———∽∾∿∾∽———

R eligion loves Matthew 7:15-23. Religion uses this to strike fear into the hearts of its followers. To be honest, it scared me for the longest time. I would think, "What if Jesus is talking about me? What if he told me, 'I never knew you'?" I remember the pain and borderline suffering this passage caused me. However, when we compare scripture with other scripture, it really is not that scary at all—unless, of course, you are a false prophet. False prophets are what this passage is about (see verse 15).

> Not every one that saith unto me, "Lord, Lord," shall enter into the kingdom of heaven; but he that doeth the will of my Father which is in heaven. Many will say to me in that day, "Lord, Lord, have we not prophesied in thy name? and in thy name have cast out devils? and in thy name done many wonderful works?" And then will I profess unto them, "I never knew you: depart from me, ye that work iniquity." (Matthew 7:21-23)

Let's start with verse 21: "but he that doeth the will of my Father". We must ask, "WHAT is the WILL of the Father?" The answer is in John 6:40, which reads,

"And this is the **will of him** that sent me, that every one which seeth the Son, and believeth on him, may have everlasting life: and I will raise him up at the last day."

Continuing on in verse 22 we read, "and in thy name done many wonderful works?" *Notice what these people were relying on to go to heaven.* They were relying on (trusting in) their **WORKS** to save them. The Bible states over and over: "**NOT by works**" (Eph 2:8,9; Titus 3:5; Rom 4:5,6; Rom 3:25-28 and my all-time favorite Rom 11:6 which reads,

"and if by grace, then is it **NO MORE OF WORKS**; otherwise grace is no more grace".

Also notice what they **DIDN'T** say. They didn't say, "Lord, I believed you paid my sin debt at the cross." Their faith was NOT in Jesus. Rather, their faith was in their works. Let's move on to verse 23 and the phrase, "I NEVER knew you". Jesus DIDN'T say, "I once knew you and now I don't." He said, "I NEVER knew you." As a result, we can conclude that these people were never saved. Jesus ate with sinners and told the Pharisees that harlots were getting into the kingdom before them (Matt 21:31). Remember the woman washing His feet with tears. The Pharisees called her a sinner. Jesus said to her, "...thy sins are forgiven... thy faith hath saved thee" (Luke 7:48-50). The point of these passages is this: **Jesus KNOWS**

sinners! This is especially true in light of the fact that the Bible says **we are ALL sinners** (Rom 3: 9-12).

The second part of verse 23 says "ye that work iniquity". Were they sinners? YES. Wait, do I work iniquity (sin)? YES. Do you still work iniquity (sin)? YES, you do. In fact, the great evangelical Paul could not stop sinning (Rom 7:14-25) We know that every person is a sinner and works iniquity. Some people commit sin more than others, but the Bible concludes **ALL** under sin (Rom 3:9-12). Saved people sin all the time in the Bible. The Bible also reads that all sins are forgiven to the believer.

"And you, being dead in your sins and the uncircumcision of your flesh, hath he quickened together with him, having forgiven you **ALL** trespasses; blotting out the handwriting of ordinances that was against us, which was contrary to us, and took it out of the way, nailing it to his cross" (Col 2:13,14).

"And by him all that believe are justified from **ALL** things, from which ye could not be justified by the law of Moses" (Acts 13:39).

"Wherefore I say unto you, **ALL** manner of sin and blasphemy shall be FORGIVEN unto men: but the blasphemy against the Holy Ghost shall not be forgiven unto men. And whosoever speaketh a word against the Son of man, it shall be forgiven him: but whosoever speaketh against the Holy Ghost, it shall not be forgiven him, neither in this world, neither in the world to come" (Matt 12:31,32).

CLOSING THOUGHTS

Many say the problem is that these professing Christians were relying on their works and not going to heaven. I believe this is a **true** statement. How many professing Christians do you know who are relying on works to help them get into heaven? However, I also see something else here. Those who fit this "mantra" are Jehovah's Witnesses and Mormons.

1. Both groups were started by a supposed prophet (Joe Smith and William Russell Taze)
2. Both groups do many wonderful works in the name of Jesus (and declare that works are needed)
3. Both groups DENY the deity of Jesus. They think he is the archangel Michael.

Jesus will say I NEVER knew you! Paul wrote in 2 Corinthians 11:3,4:

But I fear, lest by any means, as the serpent beguiled Eve through his subtilty, so your minds should be corrupted from the **simplicity** that is in Christ. For if he that cometh preacheth **another Jesus**, whom we have not preached, or if ye receive another spirit, which ye have not received, or another gospel, which ye have not accepted, ye might well bear with him.

NOTE: many versions read something completely different in 2 Cor 11:3. This is the KJV.

Jesus said in the book of John, "...unless ye believe that I am he, ye shall die in your sins" (John 8:24). One must believe in the deity of Jesus, that He is God's only Son,

God in the flesh (1 Tim 3:16; John 1:14). Any other Jesus is "another Jesus".

Whether the problem here is proclaiming works for salvation OR these folks trusting "another Jesus", they were being judged by the law and were not under grace. The born again believer is "dead to the law" (Rom 7:2-4), is not under the law (Gal 3:23-25), but under grace. The law can't touch the born again believer. IF you have trusted Jesus and His glorious gospel as your only hope to go to heaven, I can tell you with 100% certainty: Jesus KNOWS you!

Chapter 13

1 John 3:9

———〜〜〜———

"Whosoever is born of God **doth** not commit sin;
for his seed remaineth in him: and he cannot sin,
because he is born of God" (1 John 3:9).

After three years of study, I still couldn't figure this
out. Unless you know the answer to this passage, you
should be scratching your head. He that is born of God doth
not commit sin? If you know a bit of scripture, you know that
saved people commit sin. Paul couldn't stop sinning (Rom
7:14-25). The church at Corinth was completely carnal (1 Cor
3:1-3). Peter was called Satan and denied Jesus three times
after his name was written in heaven (Luke 10:20). Earlier in
1 John it was written,

"If we say that we have no sin, we deceive ourselves,
and the truth is not in us" (1 John 1:8).

I have heard of supposed contradictions in different
books, but in the same book? How can someone born of

God not commit sin? What about all these examples from the Bible of saved people sinning? Maybe the KJV is wrong. Maybe there is something missing in the translation. The ESV reads,

> "No one born of God makes a practice of sinning, for God's seed abides in him, and he cannot keep on sin-ning because he has been born of God" (1 John 3:9).

Okay, this makes more sense (**from the human perspec-tive**). However, let us check the Strong's concordance for the Greek word used. The word used means "to not commit one act of sin" (**DOTH** = *poiew*). The Strong's website gave the opposite of the word. The words opposite meant "to prac-tice sin" (*prassw*). Therefore the Greek word in 3:9 does **NOT** mean to continually practice sin. As a result, the KJV gets this right! We also know that the carnal church of Corinth did more than practice sin and they were saved. Paul practiced sin. Did I just say that? Yes I did. In the passage of Romans 7:14-25, see verse 19:

> "For the good that I would I do not: but the evil which I would not, that **I DO**."

Look in a strong concordance (go online if you don't have one) and look up the word for "**DO**". The word is *prassw*. It means to practice, to habitually commit. So we have learned that "practice sin" is a bad translation. We see that Paul prac-ticed sin. We all practice sin. *We don't understand how deep sin really goes.* Jesus said to get to heaven "BE YE **PERFECT**" (Matt 5:48). If you think you are perfect on any given day, I

suggest you check again. When bringing up the commandments for salvation, Jesus said to the rich young ruler, "If
thou wilst be **PERFECT**, sell **ALL** you have, give it to the poor
and follow me" (Luke 18:22).

Have you sold **ALL** you have, given it to the poor and
followed Jesus? If not, you are *willfully* not being "**PERFECT**"
and breaking the commandments of "thou shalt not covet"
as well as the first commandment, "thou shalt love the Lord
thy God with **ALL** thy heart, with **ALL** thy soul and with **ALL**
thy mind". Do you ever have sinful thoughts? Do you love the
Lord with **ALL** your mind? Paul understood how deep our sin
really goes. Let's get back to the verse, shall we?

> "Whosoever is born of God doth not commit sin;
> for his seed remaineth in him: and he cannot sin,
> because he is born of God" (1 John 3:9).

This is a true statement. He that is born of God doth not
commit sin; not one single act! How is this possible? The
answer is quite simple. Jesus said, "Ye must be born again"
(John 3:3). This means one must be born from above. When
Jesus says "must", I think it is probably important. Jesus
explains in verses 5 and 6.

> "Jesus answered, 'Verily, verily, I say unto thee, except
> a man be born of water AND of the Spirit, he cannot
> enter into the kingdom of God. That which **is born of
> the flesh is flesh**; and that which **is born of the Spirit
> is spirit**'" (John 3:5,6).

Do you see it? There are **two separate births**. One is born of the flesh and one is born of the Spirit. Why does one need this spirit birth? We need it because our flesh birth is not perfect. Our flesh births sins. Heaven is a perfect place; if God allowed sin into heaven; it would not be perfect anymore. As a result, we must receive this new birth. Flesh and blood cannot inherit the kingdom of God.

"Now this I say, brethren, **that flesh and blood cannot inherit the kingdom of God**; neither doth corruption inherit incorruption" (1 Cor 15:50).

If we go back a few verses, we see the two separate births.

There are also **celestial bodies**, and **bodies terrestrial**: but the glory of the celestial is one, and the glory of the terrestrial is another. There is one glory of the sun, and another glory of the moon, and another glory of the stars: for one star differeth from another star in glory. So also is the resurrection of the dead. **It is sown in corruption**; it **is raised in incorruption**: It **is sown in dishonour**; it is raised in glory: it is sown in weakness; it is raised in power: It is **sown a natural body**; it is raised **a spiritual body**. There is **a natural body**, and there is **a spiritual body.** And so it is written, the first man Adam was **made a living soul**; the last Adam was **made a quickening spirit.** Howbeit that was not first which is spiritual, **but that which is natural**; and afterward **that which is spiritual.** The first man is **of the earth**, earthy; the second man **IS OF THE LORD** from heaven.As is the earthy, such are **they also that are earthy**: and as is the heavenly, such are **they also that are heavenly.** And as we have **borne the image of the earthy**, we shall also **bear the image of the heavenly**. Now this I say, brethren, that **flesh and blood cannot inherit the kingdom of God**; neither doth corruption inherit incorruption. (1 Cor 15:40-50)

Again, do you see it? There are **two separate births** for the believer in Jesus. The first birth is of the flesh. It is from Adam. It is sown in dishonor, sown a natural body; it is of the earth. The second birth is of the Lord (verse 47). It is raised in incorruption, raised in power and made a quickening Spirit. Again: **TWO SEPARATE** births. Do we see this anywhere else in scripture? YES. We see this in Romans as well as Galatians. In Romans 7:14-25 when Paul explained he was still a sinner and hated what he did, he wrote,

"Now then it is no more I that do it, but sin that dwelleth in me" (verse 17).

Think about it for a second or two. Paul, the writer of most of the New Testament, just said it was not him that sinned, **but** the sin that was in him. How is that possible? The new man (new birth) **does not sin,** but the old man (flesh birth) still sinned—two separate births. This phenomenon also prompted Paul to write this in Galatians 5:17:

"For the **flesh lusteth against the Spirit**, and the **Spirit against the flesh**: and these are contrary the one to the other: so that ye cannot do the things that ye would."

Do you ever say or do something and think to yourself, "Why did I do that?" If you are a born again believer, this is the war that is going on inside you. The two births war against each other so that you do not always do the things that you would. Let's go back to 1 John 3:9. "Whosoever is born of God doth not commit sin; for his **seed** remaineth in him: and he cannot sin, because he is born of God." Notice: "for His seed remaineth in him". It is **this seed** that is perfect and doth not commit sin. It is **this seed** that gets to go to heaven because it is born of God. This is why one must be born again. We need this second birth that is perfect. We need this seed from God that is perfect. Our flesh birth from Adam sins; our spirit birth from our heavenly Father does not sin—**NOT ONE SINGLE ACT**! As a result, he that is born of God **TRULY** does not commit sin. How? God's seed remaineth in him. He **cannot** sin. How? He has received a **spirit birth** that does **not** sin. Two separate births. This is how saved people in the Bible still commit sin. They still have the old flesh, sinful birth from Adam (born of the flesh). However, they also have the new, perfect birth from God (born of the Spirit). Jesus said, "That which is **born of the flesh is flesh**; and that which is **born of the Spirit is Spirit**" (John 3:6). Special thanks to Ralph Yankee Arnold the best pastor on YouTube, for this answer. I highly recommend him.

Chapter 14

The Lists

—~~~—

If you have ever discussed the gospel and the plan of salvation with the "religious", you will inevitably hear the lists. What are the lists? Where are they located in the Bible? Well, the lists are a set of do's and don'ts. If you do them, you will not inherit the kingdom of God, or so the religious would like you to believe. These lists are located in 1 Corinthians 6 and Galatians 5. We will start with Corinthians as that is the easiest to explain. Then we will go the list in Galatians and determine the message Paul was trying to convey, **in context**.

> "Know ye not that the unrighteous shall not inherit the kingdom of God? Be not deceived: neither fornicators, nor idolaters, nor adulterers, nor effeminate, nor abusers of themselves with mankind, nor thieves, nor covetous, nor drunkards, nor revilers, nor extortioners, shall inherit the kingdom of God" (1 Cor 6:9,10).

Read by itself, this passage seems to contradict salvation by grace through faith in the gospel alone. If you do these things, you will not inherit the kingdom of God. However, we know the Bible **CANNOT** contradict itself. The answer is rather easy. All we need to do is keep reading. If we keep reading, the answer will become obvious.

"And such were some of you: **but** ye **are** washed, **but** ye **are** sanctified, **but** ye **are** justified in the name of the Lord Jesus, and by the Spirit of our God (1 Cor 6:11).

This verse clears up what Paul was trying to say. I want you to notice the word "**but**". "**But**" tells you there was something different about them. It does **NOT** read "BUT ye stopped doing these things". It does **NOT** read "BUT,ye don't do these things as much". It does read, "**but** ye are washed, **but** ye are sanctified, **but** ye are justified in the name of the Lord Jesus Christ." Yep, this carnal church (1 Cor 3:1-3) was washed, sanctified and justified. According to Heb 10:14, they were perfected forever. If that does not clear this passage up for you, go to the next verse.

"**ALL things are lawful unto me**, but all things are not expedient: all things are lawful for me, but I will not be brought under the power of any" (1 Cor 6:12).

How could Paul write this list saying "if you do these things then you will not inherit the kingdom of God" then turn around and declare that all things are lawful? It is simple—he can't.

Start at the beginning of the chapter 6 in Corinthians and you will see that this saved church had members who were taking each other to court. Paul was asking, "Why would you go to the unrighteous (unsaved) to settle these disputes?" Know ye not that the unrighteous (unsaved) shall not inherit the kingdom of God? "And such were some of you: **but** ye are washed, **but** ye are sanctified, **but** ye are justified in the name of the Lord Jesus, and by the Spirit of our God." We clearly see that those sins don't stop a saved person from inheriting the kingdom of God. This leads us to another list. This list is found in Galatians 5. The answer is a bit harder to see, as one needs to look at the context of the whole epistle to determine what Paul was communicating.

> Now the works of the flesh are manifest, which are these; Adultery, fornication, uncleanness, lasciviousness, idolatry, witchcraft, hatred, variance, emulations, wrath, strife, seditions, heresies, envyings, murders, drunkenness, revellings, and such like: of the which I tell you before, as I have also told you in time past, that they which do such things shall not inherit the kingdom of God. (Galatians 5:19-21)

First, as you have read this phrase many times already: the Bible **CANNOT** contradict itself. The word I want you to notice is "**strife**". Are you married? Do you argue with your spouse? Are you employed? Do you argue with your co-workers? How about your boss? Let's go back to Corinthians for a moment.

"For ye are yet carnal: for whereas there is among you
envying, and **strife**, and divisions, are ye not carnal,
and walk as men?" (1 Cor 3:3).

Alright—if those who "envy and strife" cannot inherit
the kingdom of God, how can this saved yet carnal church
at Corinth have envying and strife? How is that possible?
NO, you cannot lose your salvation (see eternal security
chapter). This can be understood when we look **at the context** of Galatians. Galatians is covered in detail in the chapter,
"Repent of your sins". It clearly shows that someone had come
unto the church at Galatia and preached another gospel.
They added the law to the gospel, thus frustrating grace (Gal
1:6-8 and Gal 2:16-21). The whole book of Galatians is about
NO LAW for salvation. IF this passage means that those that
do these things don't inherit the kingdom of God, then
Paul just contradicted himself by going against the entire
book of Galatians that he wrote, as well as the church at
Corinth having envying and strife among them. What was
Paul really saying?

Let's say that you are trying to speak with atheists **about
salvation**. You need to let them know they are sinners.
Without knowing one is a sinner, how can one realize what
he or she is being saved from? You need the law to show
people they are in trouble with God and that they need a
savior. We need to **convict** this atheist. Galatians calls the law
"our schoolmaster" to bring us to Christ. It is the same thing
here in Galatians. In context, these believers were putting
themselves **back under the law**. Paul called them **foolish** for
thinking this way (Gal 3:1-3). He was shocked that they were
so removed from the gospel (Gal 1:6). What do you do when

a born again believer mistakenly puts themselves under the law? **You convict them**. Envying, strife, and the like? Everyone does these occasionally. If this is you, know that if you have strife or envy, you will not inherit the kingdom of God, **unless** ye are washed, ye are sanctified, ye are justified by the Lord Jesus Christ. *The list was used by Paul to convict these saved believers that the law cannot save them.* He was basically saying, "Remember I told you these things while you were unbelievers."

Why, then, would you put yourself back under the law? Don't allow the religious to tell you that if do these things you will not inherit eternal life. Eternal life is a free gift (Romans 5:15-20) given to those who believe (trust) that Jesus (Gods only Son, God in the flesh) died for their sins and rose again from the dead (1 Cor 15:1-4). Are you certain you will inherit eternal life? Have you been washed, sanctified and justified?

Chapter 15

Fruit Inspectors

———∞∞∞———

Fruit inspector is a term used to describe the religious. What is fruit inspecting? Well, it is what the religious use to see if a person is saved or not. The fruits of the Spirit are listed in Galatians 5 and they are: love, joy, peace, long-suffering, gentleness, goodness, faith, meekness, temperance. The religious inspect you to see if you are bearing these fruits. If you do not, they tell you, "You must not be saved." They might also proclaim, "Fruits are the evidence of salvation; they prove you are saved." They use Matthew 7:15-20 and John 15:6 to show one is going to hell for not producing these fruits. Are the religious correct in their thoughts? Of course not. We will review both the fruits of the Spirit as well as Matthew 7 and John 15:6. First, let us put on our thinking caps and ask ourselves a few questions.

1. Can an unsaved person show love?
2. Can an unsaved person show joy?
3. Can an unsaved person show longsuffering towards humanity (through charity)?
4. Can unsaved people promote peace (Gandhi)?

If you are honest, the obvious answer is **yes** to all the questions. Let's take this a step further, shall we?

1. Do Jehovah's Witnesses show these fruits? (If you didn't know, they don't believe that Jesus was God in the flesh and think you have to earn salvation).
2. How about Mormons? Do they show fruits of the Spirit?
3. Do peace loving Muslims show any of these fruits?

Again, the answers to these questions are an astounding **YES.** Are these groups saved? **No.** If unsaved people show these fruits, and many in abundance, why does the religious use "fruits" as a gauge to determine salvation? Hmmmmmmm. Do you know who else shows these "fruits" according to the Bible? You may be surprised to learn not only unsaved people show these attributes, but also those who minister to Satan. Matthew 7, in reference to false prophets, reads:

"Beware of false prophets, which come to you **in sheep's clothing**, but inwardly they are ravening wolves" (Matt 7:15). Notice, they are outwardly sheep, thus showing "fruits of the Spirit".

We also read in 2 Corinthians 11:13 and 14:

"For such are **false apostles**, deceitful workers, **transforming themselves into the apostles of Christ**. And no marvel; for Satan himself is transformed into an angel of light."

Do you see it? False apostles transform themselves into the apostles of Christ, thus showing fruits of the Spirit. This is also true of Satan, who transforms himself into an angel of light, thus showing fruits of the Spirit.

Let's take a look at fruits from a saved perspective. The church at Corinth was carnal, but were babes **in Christ** (1 Cor 3:1-3). They were a saved church; sanctified (1:2). However, they were sinning all over the place. Some of their sins were envying, strife, and divisions (3:3). A believer has relations with his stepmother (1 Cor 5:5), there were lawsuits among the believers (1 Cor 6:7) there was fornication (1 Cor 7:2), there was drunkenness at the Lord's Supper (1 Cor 11:21). How many fruits of the Spirit were they showing? Not many, **but** they were saved.

With reason and scripture we can conclude that fruits of the Spirit are not evidence of salvation. If the unsaved can do them without the Holy Spirit and saved people can all but ignore them, why do the religious insist it is mandatory that they should be exhibited? Because that's what the "religious" do. Their mantra of "do" for salvation exceeds Jesus's "done". What about Matthew 7:15-20 and John 15:6?

> Beware of **false prophets**, which come to you in **sheep's clothing**, but inwardly they are ravening wolves. Ye shall know them by their fruits. Do men gather grapes of thorns, or figs of thistles? Even so every good tree bringeth forth good fruit; but a corrupt tree bringeth forth evil fruit. A good tree **cannot** bring forth evil fruit, **neither can** a corrupt tree bring forth good fruit. Every tree that bringeth not forth good fruit is hewn down,

and cast into the fire. Wherefore by their fruits ye shall know them. (Matthew 7:15-20).

From a first look at this passage, it appears that if one does not produce fruit, he or she is going to hell. First, this passage is about false prophets (verse 15), **not** the born again believer. Verse 16 reads, "You will know **them** (false prophets) by their fruits." Well, this is not referring to fruits of the Spirit, as Satan presents himself as an angel of light. Notice verse 18: "a good tree **cannot** bring forth evil fruit". Do you sin? Then guess what, you are not a good tree. The only good tree is Jesus. Jesus said, "Why callest me thou good? There is **none** good but God" (Luke 18:19). Then we get to verse 20, which reads, "Wherefore by their fruits you will know them." Well, if false apostles transform themselves into apostles of Christ and Satan presents himself as an angel of light, what does "fruit" mean? The answer is in Luke, which talks about the SAME thing.

For a good tree bringeth not forth corrupt fruit; neither doth a corrupt tree bring forth good fruit. For every tree is known by his own fruit. For of thorns men do not gather figs, nor of a bramble bush gather they grapes. A good man out of the good treasure of his heart bringeth forth that which is good; and an evil man out of the evil treasure of his heart bringeth forth that which is evil: for of the abundance of the heart **HIS MOUTH SPEAKETH**. (Luke 6:43-45)

This is what fruit means in this passage. It is doctrine and what that doctrine produces (**fruit**). There are only two ways to see false prophets. One, if they prophesy something and it does not come to pass then they are not from God (Duet 18:22). The second area is "what is coming out of their mouths". If you study your Bible and learn, you can tell someone is false by the words they speak. Bad doctrine, or false doctrine, will not produce for the kingdom. For example, what type of fruit were the Pharisees producing? What does Scripture teach us?

> "Woe unto you, scribes and Pharisees, hypocrites! for ye compass sea and land to make one proselyte, and when he is made, ye make him twofold more the child of hell than yourselves" (Matt 23:15).

Their **fruit** was to proclaim salvation by the works of the law to their disciples, to root their disciples in that doctrine that they **became more a child of hell then their teachers**! This was the "fruit" of the Pharisees (ClearGospel.org). As a result, we need to abide in Jesus (correct doctrine) to produce fruit (converts) for the kingdom.

This leads us to John 15:6, "If a man abide not in me, he is cast forth as a branch, and is withered; and men gather them, and cast them into the fire, and they are burned." First, what did Jesus say to do for salvation from hell? Go back to the chapter, *What Does It Mean to Believe?*. Jesus said to believe (trust) in Him for salvation. IF you have done this, you have abided in Jesus to do what was needed to have everlasting life. Remember, Jesus promised not to cast you out; He will never lose you and nothing will pluck you out of His hand (John 6:39 and John 10:28). Jesus CANNOT contradict

Himself. Second, Jesus is talking to believers (disciples). Look what he says starting in verse 3.

> Now **ye are clean** through the word which I have spoken unto you. Abide in me, and I in you. As the branch cannot bear fruit of itself, except it abide in the vine; no more can ye, except ye abide in me. I am the vine, ye are the branches: He that abideth in me, and I in him, the same bringeth forth much fruit: for without me ye can do nothing. If a man abide not in me, he is cast forth as a branch, and is withered; and men gather them, and cast them into the fire, and they are burned. If ye abide in me, and my words abide in you, ye shall ask what ye will, and it shall be done unto you. Herein is my Father glorified, that ye bear much fruit; **so shall ye be my disciples**. (John 15:3-8)

Notice verse 3: "ye are clean". These were already saved people—Jesus's disciples. Jesus then tells them that He is the vine and that they can produce nothing without Him. However, there is that word "fire" again... but do you remember Jesus's promises? He promised to not cast you out and to never lose you. As a result, the already saved disciples could NOT go to hell. What, then, is this "fire" spoken about? A word may have different meanings based on context.

1. Baptism can refer to water, fire, Holy Spirit
2. Judgment can refer to hell, God's discipline or the judgment seat of Christ
3. Saved (delivered) can refer to hell, God's wrath, temporal death
4. Dead can mean unsaved or useless.

We **cannot** assume the meaning of this verse means being cast into hell just because the word "fire" is used. We clearly see that salvation is **FREE** (Rom 5:15-20; Eph 2:8,9; Rom 3:24-28, Rom 6:23). IF it's free, then it can't be a "trade" for fruit bearing. Another question—how much fruit did the thief on the cross bear? None.

THE MEANING

Jesus uses this as an "idiom" or metaphor. IF one does not abide in him, he or she is "useless". Useless branches are tossed away. This does not mean saved people can go to hell. That would contradict so many passages of scripture. Jesus is just saying that if you don't abide in him (to bear fruit), then you are as useless as a branch bearing no fruit and will be set aside. In other words **"God won't use you"**. Can a believer produce no fruit and go to heaven? **YES**. The Bible is clear. Salvation is by grace through faith in the gospel of Jesus. In 1 Cor 3:11-15 we read how we, as born again believers, will stand before the judgment seat of Christ, where our works will be tested for reward. Some will have all their works burnt up, but they themselves will be saved. If they had "borne fruit", that fruit would not have been burnt up, but rewarded. We conclude with verse 8, which tells us the context of the passage. Salvation is NOT in view here. Discipleship is in view here: "so shall ye be my disciples". Salvation and discipleship—always keep them separate.

For salvation, Jesus said, "Come unto me, all ye that labour and are heavy laden, and I will give you **rest**. Take my yoke upon you, and learn of me; for I am meek and lowly in heart: and ye shall find rest unto your souls. For my yoke is **easy**, and my burden is light" (Matt 11:28-30). For discipleship (service) Jesus said "pick up your cross and follow me". Discipleship is **NOT** easy with a light burden. They are talking about two different things. The religious confuse salvation and discipleship; please don't make the same mistake. Salvation is FREE. Discipleship is costly, BUT will be rewarded at the Judgment Seat of Christ. If you abide in Him, you can bear much fruit! Are you in the doctrine of Jesus or the doctrine of the Pharisees (religion)? The parable of the publican and the Pharisee is a great illustration for this chapter.

And he spake this parable unto certain which **trusted in themselves** that they were righteous, and despised others: "Two men went up into the temple to pray; the **one a Pharisee**, and the other a publican. The Pharisee stood and prayed thus with himself, '**God, I thank thee**, that I am **not** as other men are, extortioners, unjust, adulterers, or even as this publican. I **fast twice in the week, I give tithes** of all that I possess.' And the publican, standing afar off, would not lift up so much as his eyes unto heaven, but smote upon his breast, saying, '**God be merciful to me a sinner.**' I tell you, this man went down to his house justified **rather** than the other: for every one that exalteth himself shall be abased; and he that humbleth himself shall be exalted." (Luke 18:9-14)

What should we take away from THIS parable?
1. The Pharisee "trusted in himself", that he was righteous. (verse 9)
2. The Pharisee actually gave credit to God. (verse 11)

3. He had good works. He fasted and tithed. (verse 12)
4. Was the Pharisee showing "fruit" by his works? According to religion's definition, YES he was.
5. The publican simply asked for mercy, admitting he was a sinner.
6. The Pharisee was **NOT** justified (see the word **rather** in verse 14), but the publican was justified.

With regards to FRUIT, of the two (Pharisee and publican), who was showing more fruit?

RELIGION would say, "**the Pharisee**". However, the Pharisee left **UNJUSTIFIED**.

As a result of the passages shown in this chapter, we can conclude...

1. Fruit is not needed for salvation.
2. Fruit is not always fruits of the Spirit, as the unsaved can show these fruits.
3. Fruit can be bad, as the fruit of the Pharisees sent people to hell.
4. Fruit is NOT the evidence of salvation, as Satan presents himself as an angel of light.
5. Fruit is not produced by EVERY Christian (see 1 Cor 3:11-15).

Chapter 16

Examine yourself

———⌘———

"Examine yourselves, whether ye be in the faith, prove
your own selves. Know ye not your own selves, how
that Jesus Christ is in you, except ye be reprobates"
(2 Cor 13:5).

Often this verse is used by the religious to have a person
examine his or her self to determine whether he or she
is a "real" Christian. Are you doing works, sinning less, going
to church, tithing, partaking in sacraments, etc? Are you performing these things? If not, the religious will proclaim, "You
are probably not a real Christian." You know, because the
religious are superior to all other sinners. They have "proved"
their faith. "Look at this wonderful fruit coming from me."
However, in reality, the scriptures prove a person's salvation.
It is not by works we do (Titus 3:5). *If salvation is not of ourselves, according to Eph 2:8,9, then why should we examine
ourselves to see if one is saved?* We shouldn't. What then, is
this passage telling us? It is quite simple actually. We need to
go back a few verses and look at the context. What you will

see is this: these saved Corinthians were questioning Paul's apostleship. Go back a few verses.

> *"...since ye seek a proof of Christ speaking in me,* which to you ward is not weak, but is mighty in you" (2 Cor 13:3).

These saved people were looking for proof of Paul's apostleship. As a result, Paul was pretty much saying, "You seek proof of my apostleship. You want to examine me? You need to examine yourself to see if you are in the faith." This was a simple tit for tat. Notice Paul ends this very short "spat" in the very next verse. "But I trust that ye shall **know** that **we** are **not** reprobates" (2 Cor 13:6). The sequence of verses is pretty straight forward.

1. They questioned Paul's apostleship.
2. Paul said they should examine themselves to see if they were reprobates.
3. Paul immediately follows that by stating, "But I trust that ye shall know, that we are not reprobates."

Paul never told them to "examine" themselves to see if they were really saved. We already have seen that things we do don't prove salvation (chapter on fruit-inspectors). If Paul wanted them to really examine themselves, wouldn't he quickly give us a list to look at to determine our salvation? He would, but there is no criteria given in this chapter. As a result, we can conclude that the religious twist this passage to fit their "works for salvation" doctrine.

If you are "examining" yourself for evidence to prove you are saved, stop it! It is very dangerous to do so. Peter was walking on water. When he started to examine himself and his surroundings, he sank. Examine yourself to see if you are living the Christian life that you **should** be living that is pleasing to God? YES. Simply keep reading in this passage. Examine yourself to see if you are a "real" Christian? **NO**. When it comes to salvation from hell, the only thing one needs to examine is his or her faith. Is your faith really in Jesus (God's only Son; God in the flesh)? Have you believed the gospel, that Jesus died for all your sins and rose again? Do you believe that all your sins were dealt with (paid) at the cross and you have no sins left to send you to hell? If so, there is no need to examine yourself _**for**_ salvation.

Chapter 17

Go and sin no more

———༄༅༄———

"Go and sin no more" is the gospel of the sinless perfectionist. We have already seen that this is not the gospel. We know that the gospel is declared in 1 Cor 15:1-4. What, then, are we supposed to get from this phrase? What was Jesus trying to tell us? Most people pull this phrase from the woman caught in adultery.

> "When Jesus had lifted up himself, and saw none but the woman, he said unto her, 'Woman, where are those thine accusers? Hath no man condemned thee?' She said, 'No man, Lord.' And Jesus said unto her, 'Neither do I condemn thee: **go, and sin no more**'" (John 8:10,11).

Jesus did say these words. It is undeniable. It is in the Bible. However, not to be disrespectful to the Lord, I have to ask the million dollar question: go and sin no more... or what will happen? Every saved person sinned after they were saved (one could argue the thief on the cross, we will call that semantics). Peter denied Jesus and didn't uphold the gospel AFTER salvation (Gal 2:11-14). Paul couldn't stop all his sinning (Rom 7:15-25) and he was already saved. The carnal people at Corinth were sinning all over the place and they were saved (1 Cor 3:1-3).

The answer to the million dollar question is given by Jesus himself. What most people miss is that Jesus said this to another person, another whom He healed.

> "Afterward Jesus findeth him in the temple, and said unto him, 'Behold, thou art made whole: sin no more, **lest a worse thing come unto thee'**" (John 5: 14).

There we have our answer to the question. The answer is, "lest something worse thing come upon thee". Jesus is telling us that sin does have its consequences. The Bible is clear on this. Some of these consequences include:

- Loss of joy (Psalm 51:12)
- Loss of rewards at the Judgment Seat of Christ (1 Cor 3:10-15)
- Being called least in the Kingdom (matt 5:19)
- Being ashamed at His appearing (1 John 2:28)
- Being a vessel of DIS-honor (2 Tim 2:20-21)
- Satan could have access to your flesh (1 Cor 5:5)
- Being disciplined by God (Heb 12:5-6)
- Having your physical life taken early (Acts 5: 1-11)
- Be made sick by God (1 Cor 11:30-32)

How about consequences from the law here on earth? This applies to the woman caught in adultery. Jesus told her "go and sin no more". Why did He say this? Lest something worse would happen unto her. In those days, the law stated that one would be stoned if caught in adultery. If she committed that sin again, she could actually be stoned. This is much worse than having Jesus save her from being stoned.

Jesus **NEVER** said...

- Go and sin no more or you can't go to heaven
- Go and sin no more or you will lose your salvation
- Go and sin no more or you will be cast out

Don't let religion tell you these things. They are simply not true.

What Jesus said was, "Go and sin no more, lest a worse thing come unto thee."

Chapter 18

Is water baptism a requirement for salvation?

———∽∾∿∾∽———

W ater baptism does have its place in the faith. The Bible talks about this often. Both Jews and Gentiles alike were baptized after receiving the **free gift** of salvation. Peter and the other apostles baptized AFTER conversion. Paul, with his ministers baptized after salvation (the jailer and the Ethiopian). However, it is **not** a requirement for salvation from hell. One of the main verses used to place baptism as a requirement is Acts 2:38.

> "Then Peter said unto them, 'Repent, and be baptized every one of you in the name of Jesus Christ for the remission of sins, and ye shall receive the gift of the Holy Ghost.'"

As always, let us use scripture to interpret scripture and we shall see what the Word says. We will start with John the Baptist. Several of the gospels tell of John the Baptist and his water baptizing. He was baptizing with water *unto* repentance. However, John the Baptist said, "there is one that cometh after me that will baptize you with the Holy Spirit" (Matt 3:11). It is the baptism of the Holy Spirit that saves, not water.

Salvation from hell is a **free gift** (Rom 5:15-20, Rom 3:24-28, Rom 6:23) and salvation is not of works. If we need to get water baptized to enter heaven, then salvation is partially of ourselves and works.

"For it is by grace ye are saved through faith, it is NOT of yourselves, it is the GIFT of God, **not of works**, lest any man should boast" (Eph 2:8,9).

"And if by grace, then **is it no more of works**: otherwise grace is no more grace. But if it be of works, then it is no more grace: otherwise work is no more work" (Rom 11:6*).*

If salvation is a free gift, then it cannot be a contract contingent on water baptism. In case there is any concern over what is work, let's look at the Greek word for "work" and see what the biblical definition of a work is. The Greek word for work is *ergon*. The definition is as follows.

Strong's #2041: ergon (pronounced er'-gon)
—from a primary (but obsolete) ergo (to work); toil (as an effort or occupation); by implication, **AN ACT:**—deed, doing, labor, work

Is water baptism "an act" performed by man? **Yes it is**. It is therefore considered a work. We clearly see that salvation is not of works. Salvation is either by grace or by works as *one eliminates the other* (Rom 11:6).

Was there ever a person who was "filled with the Holy Ghost" before water baptism? Yes, there were several. One such example is in Acts 10. Cornelius, who feared God but was not saved, and his group were filled with the Holy Ghost before being water baptized.

> While Peter yet spake these words, the Holy Ghost fell on all them which heard the word. And they of the circumcision which believed were astonished, as many as came with Peter, because that on the Gentiles also was poured out the gift of the Holy Ghost. For they heard them speak with tongues, and magnify God. THEN answered Peter, "Can any man forbid water, that these should not be baptized, which have received the Holy Ghost as well as we." (Acts 10:44-47)

This group was **not** baptized with water yet, BUT they had already received the Holy Ghost. Thus the argument that water baptism was (is) a necessity to receive the Holy Ghost is **not** correct. If one must be baptized to receive the Holy Ghost, how was it possible for this group? How then does one receive the Holy Spirit?

According to Paul, a person is **SEALED** by the Holy Spirit when he or she believes (trusts) in the gospel (Eph 1:13,14). If one is sealed by the Holy Spirit at belief, where is water baptism in that? One might argue that baptism is part of the gospel. You have read the gospel and know it is declared in 1 Cor 15:1-4. We will also see that Paul differentiates baptism from the gospel.

"For Christ sent me **not** to baptize, **BUT** to preach the gospel: not with wisdom of words, lest the cross of Christ should be made of none effect" (1 Cor 1:17).

"I thank God that I baptized none of you, but Crispus and Gaius; Lest any should say that I had baptized in mine own name" (1 Cor 1:14-15).

It is Jesus and Him crucified that has the power to save— NOT water. For those who think water baptism is part of the gospel, Paul clearly separates baptism and the gospel in 1 Cor 1:17. Here are some other passages to consider when talking about water baptism.

"The like figure whereunto even baptism doth also now save us (**not the putting away of the filth of the flesh**, but the answer of a good conscience toward God) by the resurrection of Jesus Christ" (1 Peter 3:21).

"And such were some of you: but **ye are washed**, but ye are sanctified, but ye are justified in the name of the Lord Jesus, and **by the Spirit of our God**" (1 Cor 6:11).

We clearly see that with these verses, that baptism is the means of salvation, BUT not water baptism (putting away the filth of the flesh). Salvation is that one is baptized and washed **by the Spirit** of our God. Since we are saved by faith in the gospel of Jesus alone, let us now examine Acts 2:38.

"Then Peter said unto them, 'Repent, and be baptized every one of you in the name of Jesus Christ for the remission of sins, and ye shall receive the gift of the Holy Ghost.'"

We have already seen that "repent" means a change of mind. If you read earlier in Acts 2, you will see Peter convicting his Jewish audience. He was explaining to them that they just crucified their promised Messiah (Acts 2:36). These people needed to "change their minds" about who Jesus was and what He has done. It is the changing of the mind and their belief that grants the remission of sins (**Acts 2:41**). It is like saying, "Repent (believe) and ye shall receive the remission of sins." Notice, the other part of the passage is between two commas. It is this part we will analyze next.

"...and be baptized every one of you in the name of Jesus Christ "for" the remission of sins..."

Many read this part and define the word "for" to mean "in order to get". As a result, they see this passage to read, "And be baptized every one of you in the name of Jesus Christ in order to get the remission of sins.

However, the word "for" does not always mean "in order to". Here is another sentence with the word "for": "Take two aspirin for your headache." If "for" takes on the meaning of "in order to get", then the sentence would read, "Take two aspirin in order to get a headache." Do you know anyone who takes two aspirin in order to get a headache? In this example, the word "for" means "because of". Take two aspirin "because of" your headache. Now, take this definition to Acts 2:38.

> "Repent (change your mind and believe), (comma) and be baptized every one of you in the name of Jesus Christ BECAUSE OF the remission of sins, (comma) and ye shall receive the gift of the Holy Ghost."

We are commanded to get baptized *because* we have received the remission of sins, *not in order to get* remission of sins. Keep reading in Acts. Acts 3 is the same scenario.

> "Repent ye therefore, and be converted, that your sins may be blotted out, when the times of refreshing shall come from the presence of the Lord" (Acts 3:19).

Hopefully you see what is being said in Acts 2:38. I have to admit—I found it difficult to explain it on paper. I had to define repent, illustrate the context of the verse, and show the commas that dictate a different thought, then explain another definition for the word "for" and tie it all together. We can conclude that water baptism is not necessary for salvation. Salvation is a free gift. Salvation is not of works—including an act. Some were filled with the Holy Ghost before baptism. We receive the Holy Spirit—we are sealed—after we believe the gospel. The gospel is separate from baptism. Although water baptism is not a requirement for salvation, it certainly has its place in the Christian faith. Should a born again believer be baptized? Yes; it is part of the great commission, a step of obedience. However, let us **NOT** diminish the **"once for ALL"** sacrifice of Jesus by adding to the gospel.

Thank you Jesus for your amazing gift! My salvation is based solely on what you accomplished, not by any act I did or will ever do. Do you truly trust in Jesus and the gospel to take you to heaven OR do you trust in your water baptism?

Chapter 19

Roman Catholicism

———*ᴄᴠᴠ*———

S ince we have reviewed many different Protestant doctrines and beliefs, in this chapter we will review some
of the doctrines of Roman Catholicism. We will look at some
of the beliefs and practices of this religion and compare it
to what the Bible reads. I am not saying that I am righteous,
as ALL we like sheep have gone astray; we have turned
everyone to his own way and the LORD hath laid on him
the iniquity of us all (Isaiah 53:6). However, my intent is to
contrast and compare between Catholicism and the Bible...
Jesus vs Religion.

THE 10 COMMANDMENTS

The 10 Commandments are as basic to the Bible as food
is to the body. Jesus said, "If you love me, you will keep
my commandments." Although keeping his commandments
is not necessary for salvation, they are a guide to how a
Christian is supposed to live. If you analyze the Roman
Catholic 10 Commandments and compare them to the Bible,

you will notice that one is MISSING. It's the second commandment, "Thou shalt NOT make unto thee any graven images... of anything in heaven above or the earth beneath... thou shalt NOT bow down to them" (Exodus 20:4,5). Walk into a Catholic church and you will see many, many statues and idols (such as Mary). You will also see many bowing to them. What the Vatican has done to the 10 Commandments is this: they have taken the commandment of "thou shalt not covet" and made two different coveting commandments (9 and 10) while removing the second commandment. Read Exodus 20 for the listing of the commandments.

NAME OF THE POPE/PRIESTS

A name used for the Pope is, "The most holy father". If you walk into a Catholic church, you will hear any person of the congregation address the pastor as "father ". This is very inappropriate. The Bible states, "And call **no man** your father upon the earth, for one is your Father, which is in heaven" (Matthew 23:9). This confirms that spiritually calling any man "father" is theologically incorrect. Yes, you CAN call your biological dad "father".

PURGATORY

One of the major doctrines of the Roman Catholic Church is the doctrine of purgatory. Purgatory is a place (after death) where Catholics go to get unrepentant sins purged or burned before entering heaven. Today, a Catholic can purchase Mass cards to help dead relatives get out of purgatory quicker. According to the Bible, purgatory doesn't exist. Paul stated,"

We are confident, I say, and willing rather to be absent from the body, and to be present with the Lord" (2 Corinthians 5:8).

When believers are absent from the body, they are present with the Lord. A very good example of this is the thief on the cross. He didn't receive salvation until his last few hours on this earth. According to Catholicism, he should have spent a long time in purgatory. However, he did not. Jesus said to the thief, "Verily I say unto thee, **today** shalt thou be with me in paradise." The thief spent **no time** in purgatory. The big issue with purgatory is simply this—if a person believes in purgatory, he or she is saying that Jesus's sacrifice was not good enough to cover his or her sins. This is to say to our Father in heaven, "The sacrifice of your Son was NOT good enough." I wonder what His reaction would be to that statement. Matthew 26:28 reads,

> "For this is my blood of the new testament, which is shed for many for the REMISSION of sins."

The Greek word for "remission" is *afesi*.
Pronounce: af'-es-is
- Strongs Number: G859
    1) release from bondage or imprisonment
    2) forgiveness or pardon, of sins (**letting them go as if they had never been committed**), remission of the penalty

Once you have put your faith in the gospel of Jesus Christ, your sins are totally forgiven as if they have never been committed. What sins does the believer have that need to be purged in purgatory? Why would one have to get certain sins purged if Jesus, by Himself, purged our sins.

> Who being the brightness of his glory, and the express image of his person, and upholding all things by the word of his power, when he had **by himself purged our sins**, sat down on the right hand of the Majesty on high (Heb 1:3)

DOCTRINES OF MARY

There are many doctrines (beliefs) concerning Mary and her role in the Catholic Church. Some of these doctrines include:

1. Mary is worthy of praise and worship
2. Mary is a co-redeemer with Jesus
3. Mary was sinless
4. Mary never had relations with her husband and no other children

All of these doctrines have no biblical support. In fact, the Bible contradicts these beliefs. Mary is not God and has no place for our worship. Christians have one redeemer—that is Christ. Mary was a sinner. Mary was faithful to her husband and they produced other offspring.

1. With prayers such as the Rosary and the bowing down to "Mary" statues, she receives ample worship from many. Luke 11:27, 28 tells us, "And it came to pass, as he spake these things, a certain woman of the company lifted up her voice, and said unto him, 'Blessed is the womb that bare

thee, and the paps which thou hast sucked.' But he said, 'Yea **rather**, blessed are they that hear the word of God, and keep it.'" A note on the rosary and prayers with vain repetition: the Bible reads, "But when ye pray, use not vain repetitions, as the heathen do: for they think that they shall be heard for their much speaking" (Matt 6:7). Prayer should be from the heart.

2. The belief that Mary is a co-redeemer with Jesus is incorrect. 1 Tim 2:5 reads, "For there is one God, and **one** mediator between God and men, the man Christ Jesus."

3. Was Mary sinless? In Luke 1:47, Mary said, "And my spirit hath rejoiced in God **my Saviour**." **ONLY** sinners need saviors. The Bible also states that ALL have sinned and fallen short of the glory of God (Rom 3:23). Does **ALL** include Mary? Yes it does.

4. Mary had "relations" with Joseph after the birth of Jesus. They had several children together. Luke 2:7 reads, "And she brought forth her *firstborn* son, and wrapped him in swaddling clothes, and laid him in a manger; because there was no room for them in the inn." "First born" tells us they had other children. We see this in several places in the Bible. One such place is in Luke 8:20, which reads, "And it was told him by certain which said, 'Thy mother and thy brethren stand without, desiring to see thee.'" See also Matthew 13:5 and Galatians 1:19.

WHORE OF BABYLON IN REVELATION 17 AND 18

The whore of Babylon in Revelation has been debated for years. The possibilities are literal Babylon, the United States, Jerusalem, and the Vatican. Babylon and the United States can easily be thrown out as possibilities. This leaves the other two. There are many Bible verses that support Jerusalem as the whore. This cannot be dismissed. However, there are several clues that don't fit. **All** clues can be connected to the Vatican. Below are some of the clues the Bible gives.

1. The woman who rides the beast is called the whore of Babylon. A woman in Bible prophecy often represents a church. Believers are known as the "bride" of Christ. This is an apostate church.

2. The woman sits on seven hills. Roman is known as the city on seven hills. The Catholic Encyclopedia also backs this claim.

3. The woman is called that great CITY. She is a city, thus eliminating the United States.

4. She is dressed in scarlet and purple. The Vatican Bishops and Cardinals are dressed in scarlet and purple.

5. She is drunk with the blood of the martyrs and the saints. Throughout history no more blood has been shed than that of the Catholic Inquisitions. Protestants were murdered by the millions.

6. The woman is decked with gold and precious stones. The Vatican is extremely rich. Her leaders are often arrayed with precious stones.

7. She holds a golden cup in her hand. When performing the "Eucharist", the Catholic Church holds up a golden cup. It is their policy that the cup be golden or plated in gold.

8. Reigns over the kings of the earth. Examine a little history and you will see that the Vatican has ruled over or with the kings of the earth.

Although I don't believe the Vatican is Christian, I do believe there are Christians in the Roman Catholic Church. Jesus says after the description of the whore, "Come out of her **MY** people." Jesus has people in the Roman Catholic system.

MUSLIMS WILL GO TO HEAVEN

This is according to the Vatican. The Bible is clear. He who hath the SON hath life; he who hath NOT the son hath NOT life. Muslims believe Jesus was a prophet. They also believe that he WASN'T crucified, that it was really someone else in his place. Why does the Vatican believe that Muslims are going to heaven? MOST Roman Catholics don't know this. The Catechism of the Roman Catholic Church reads,

> "841 The Church's relationship with the Muslims. The plan of salvation also includes those who acknowledge the Creator, in the first place amongst whom are the Muslims; these profess to hold the faith of Abraham, and together with us they adore the one, merciful God, mankind's judge on the last day."

If this were true, it would mean that one can deny Jesus and his crucifixion and obtain salvation. Jesus said, "I am the way, the truth and the life, NO MAN cometh to the Father but through ME."

OTHER MISCELLANEOUS FALSE DOCTRINES

1. Catholic priests are not allowed to marry. The Bible states in 1 Timothy 4:1-3,

Now the Spirit speaketh expressly, that in the latter times some shall depart from the faith, giving heed to seducing spirits, and **doctrines of devils**, speaking lies in hypocrisy; having their conscience seared with a hot iron; forbidding to marry, and commanding to abstain from meats, which God hath created to be received with thanksgiving of them which believe and know the truth."

This begs the question—if Peter was the first Pope (which he was not), then why was he married?!

2. The Catholics canonize "saints" after death. The Bible calls all believers saints. E.g. "Paul, an apostle of Jesus Christ by the will of God, to the *saints* which are at Ephesus, and to the faithful in Christ Jesus..." (Ephesians 1:1). Paul addresses other churches this way as well.

3. The Catholic Church says that "works" are needed for salvation. Eph 2:8,9 says, "For by grace ye are saved through faith, it is not of yourselves, it is the gift of God, **NOT OF WORKS**, least any man should boast."

It is **NOT** my intent to degrade Roman Catholics. I love them. My family has many Roman Catholics in it. My daughter's soccer team had many Roman Catholic families. It is my intent to illustrate some of their doctrine and compare it to the Bible, to illustrate the discrepancies of the teachings provided by the Vatican and the Catholic Church. Again, there are saved Catholics. Jesus said, "Come out of her MY people." This simply means He has people within this religion. However, similar to much of Protestantism, most are not truly trusting the gospel.

"**ALL** we like sheep have gone astray; we have turned everyone to his own way; and the LORD hath laid on him the iniquity of us all" (Isaiah 53:6).

The Bible says, "The wages of sin is death". Because of our sin, we are condemned to hell. As a FREE gift, God sent his only begotten Son (God in the Flesh) to pay for YOUR/MY sin (see chapter The Gospel). The moment you put your trust in that payment God seals you (Eph 1:13,14). God's plan to keep you out of hell (paying the debt you owe for your sin) is so simple. "BELIEVE on the Lord Jesus Christ and thou shalt be saved" (Acts 16:31).

Chapter 20

Some Random Verses

—⟨∿∿⟩—

B elow are some random verses I thought you might enjoy. I am going to ask this question twice. I will ask it once in the beginning of this chapter and once at the end. The question is this, "How many times does the Bible HAVE TO tell us that we are saved (justified) by grace, faith, belief in Jesus BEFORE professing Christians will actually believe it?" Romans 3:22: Even the righteousness of God which is **by faith of Jesus Christ** unto all and upon all them that believe: for there is no difference.

Romans 3:27,28: Where is boasting then? It is excluded. By what law? of works? Nay: but by the law of faith. Therefore we conclude that **a man is justified by faith** without the deeds of the law.

Romans 3:30: Seeing it is one God, which shall justify the circumcision **by faith**, and uncircumcision **through faith**.

Romans 4:5: But to him that worketh not, but believeth on him that justifieth the ungodly, **his faith is counted for righteousness.**

Romans 4:13: For the promise, that he should be the heir of the world, was not to Abraham, or to his seed, through the law, but **through the righteousness of faith.**

Romans 5:1–Therefore **being justified by faith**, we have peace with God through our Lord Jesus Christ:

Romans 9:30: What shall we say then? That the Gentiles, which followed not after righteousness, have attained to righteousness, even **the righteousness which is of faith.**

Galatians 2:16: Knowing that a man is not justified by the works of the law, but **by the faith of Jesus Christ**, even we have believed in Jesus Christ, that we might **be justified by the faith of Christ**, and not by the works of the law: for by the works of the law shall no flesh be justified.

Galatians 3:8: And the scripture, foreseeing that God would justify the heathen **through faith**, preached before the gospel unto Abraham, saying, In thee shall all nations be blessed.

Galatians 3:14: That the blessing of Abraham might come on the Gentiles through Jesus Christ; that we might receive the promise of the Spirit **through faith.**

Philippians 3:9: and be found in him, not having mine own righteousness, which is of the law, but that which is through the faith of Christ, the righteousness which is of **God by faith.**

Acts 26:18: To open their eyes, and to turn them from darkness to light, and from the power of Satan unto God, that they may receive forgiveness of sins, and inheritance among them which **are sanctified by faith** that is in me (Jesus's words).

Ephesians 2:8,9: For **by grace** are ye saved **through faith**; and that not of yourselves: it is the gift of God: Not of works, lest any man should boast.

Ephesians 1:7: In whom we have redemption through his blood, the forgiveness of sins, according to the riches of **his grace.**

Acts 15:11: But we believe that through the **grace** of the LORD Jesus Christ we shall be saved, even as they.

Romans 3:24: Being justified **freely by his grace** through the redemption that is in Christ Jesus:

Romans 4:16: Therefore **it is of faith**, that it might be **by grace**; to the end the promise might be sure to all the seed; not to that only which is of the law, but to that also which is **of the faith** of Abraham; who is the father of us all...

Romans 11:5,6: Even so then at this present time also there is a remnant according to the election of grace. And if **by grace**, then is it **no more of works**: otherwise grace is no more grace. But if it be of works, then it is no more grace: otherwise work is no more work.

Romans 5:21: That as sin hath reigned unto death, even so might **grace** reign through righteousness unto eternal life by Jesus Christ our Lord.

John 3:15,16: That whosoever **believeth in him** should not perish, but have eternal life. For God so loved the world, that he gave his only begotten Son, that whosoever **believeth in him** should not perish, but have everlasting life.

John 6:47: Verily, verily, I say unto you, He that **believeth on me** hath everlasting life.

John 11:25: I am the resurrection, and the life: he that **believeth in me**, though he were dead, yet shall he live.

Romans 1:16: For I am not ashamed of the gospel of Christ: for it is the power of God unto salvation to everyone that **believeth.**

Galatians 3:6: Even as Abraham **believed** God, and it was accounted to him for righteousness.

Romans 4:24: But for us also, to whom it shall **be imputed**, if we **believe** on him that raised up Jesus our Lord from the dead.

I think you get the point. The question is, "How many times does the Bible HAVE TO tell us that we are saved (justified) by grace, faith, belief in Jesus BEFORE professing Christians will actually believe it?" "And brought them out, and said, 'Sirs, what must **I do to be saved**?' And they said, 'Believe on the Lord Jesus Christ, and thou shalt be saved'" (Acts 16:30,31). Put your faith (trust) in Jesus and His glorious gospel alone for salvation. Do not put your faith (trust) in anything else? How many times does the Bible have to tell us? Even still, religion can blind us all.

Chapter 21

Should Do

———⟨❀⟩———

The focus of this book was to review and explain scripture that the "religious" use to deny salvation through faith in the gospel of Jesus alone. **No** works, **no** law keeping, **no** repenting of sins, **no** church affiliation, **no** sacraments— nothing but faith **in the blood** of Jesus provides forgiveness of sins (1 Pet 1:19). However, I did want to write a little bit on what a born again Christian **should** do. This is not to "earn" salvation. That is a **free gift**. This is what a Christian should do *as a result of* salvation. There is a big difference.

THE LAW

It is clear that we are not justified by the law. The law makes faith void. The law frustrates grace. If you have to keep one law, you are responsible to keep the whole law. As a result, there is no law for salvation. Does this mean that the born again believer should go around sinning all over the place? Absolutely not! In Romans 7 we read,

For the woman which hath an husband is bound by the law to her husband so long as he liveth; but if the husband be dead, she is loosed from the law of her husband. So then if, while her husband liveth, she be married to another man, she shall be called an adulteress: but if her husband be dead, she is **free from that law**; so that she is no adulteress, though she be married to another man. Wherefore, my brethren, **ye also are become dead to the law** by the body of Christ; that ye **should** be married to another, even to him who is raised from the dead, that we **should** bring forth fruit unto God. For when we were in the flesh, the motions of sins, which were by the law, did work in our members to bring forth fruit unto death. But now **we are delivered from the law**, that being dead wherein we were held; that we **SHOULD SERVE** in newness of spirit, and not in the oldness of the letter. (Romans 7:2-6)

The Bible is pretty clear again. Yes, we are "dead to the law". The law can't touch the born again believer. However, we *should serve* by establishing the law. Again—no law for salvation! However, establish the law the best you can *to serve* Jesus *because of* the free gift that He gave you. It is what we should do. It is our reasonable service (Romans 12:1).

WORKS

It is also clear that there are no works for salvation. Works eliminates grace (Rom 11:6). We are justified without works (Roman 4:1-6). No works for salvation. Does this mean we shouldn't do any good works? Absolutely not! In Ephesians 2:8-10 we read,

> "For by grace are ye saved through faith; and that not of yourselves: it is the gift of God: Not of works, lest any man should boast. For we are his workmanship, created in Christ Jesus unto good works, which God hath before ordained that we **SHOULD** walk in them."

God has already ordained that the born again believer **should** do good works. However, are they required? NOPE. Salvation is by grace through faith in the gospel. Should the believer do good works? YES. This is not to "merit" salvation, but because we are already saved. James 2 is about convicting already saved people to do good works, for they are profitable. Where are they profitable? Every believer WILL stand before the Judgment Seat of Christ, where one's "works" will be tested for a **reward**.

> For other foundation can no man lay than that is laid, which is **Jesus Christ.** Now if any man build upon this foundation gold, silver, precious stones, wood, hay, stubble; Every man's work shall be made manifest: for the day shall declare it, because it shall be revealed by fire; and the fire shall **try every man's work** of what sort it is. If any man's work abide which he hath built thereupon, **he shall receive a reward.** If any man's work shall be burned, he shall suffer loss: **but he himself shall be saved**; yet so as by fire. (1 Cor 3:11-15)

If you have believed (trusted) in the gospel of Jesus, that Christ **died for all your sins** and rose again from the dead, you are saved. It is a **done** deal. You are secure forever. Now you have a choice. Will you serve Him? Do you really want to go to the Judgment Seat of Christ and have nothing to show for what He has **done** for you? I have repeatedly brought up the carnal church at Corinth. Paul also wrote this in 1 Corinthians 6:20, "For ye are bought with a price: therefore glorify God in your body, and in your spirit, which are God's." We see that this carnal church "was bought". It is clear. They were saved. "Therefore" means "because of" or "resulting from". As a result, it reads like this: *because you are bought, glorify God.*

SHOULD an already saved person perform works for the Lord? YES
SHOULD an already saved person refrain from sinning as much as possible? YES
SHOULD an already saved person serve God? YES
SHOULD an already saved person be water baptized? YES
SHOULD an already saved person read his or her Bible and continue to grow? YES
SHOULD an already saved person spend time with like-minded believers? YES
SHOULD an already saved person abide in Jesus to produce fruit? YES

Because you are already saved, serve him the best you can with the sinful nature you possess. It is not a requirement for salvation. However, it is what the believer **should** do.

Chapter 22

Elected?

—◆◆◆—

This topic has caused much confusion. I am not going to get into all five areas (TULIP) in Calvinism. I do reject all five points. However, the only damnable one is the "P", which stands for "perseverance of the saints". The damnable doctrine of Lordship Salvation appears to have come from this. This implies works for salvation. However, I have met folks who believe in the doctrine of election that **dismiss** "perseverance of the saints". They reject any notion that works or law keeping has anything to do with salvation. I believe these folks are saved. This is similar to one who does not believe in the pre-70th week rapture but believes we are saved by grace through faith alone. Does their belief or disbelief in a pre-70th week rapture eliminate salvation? NO. Neither does believing in election. However, this **horrible** doctrine of "perseverance of the saints" is derived from election.

For example, if we are "automatically" elected by God for salvation without choice, then we will "automatically" have works. This is one of the **real dangers** of the election doctrine. I believe it is 100% false. It is wrong! Below is a paper

I wrote for someone who was considering this doctrine. As a result, it is a bit caddy.

It was once written, when a believer is about to enter into heaven, the sign on the gate would read, "Whosoever will may come". Once they enter heaven, the sign on the back-side of the gate would read, "Chosen from the foundation of the world". This is music to the ears of all Christians. How wonderful that God has chosen us to be saved, to be part of the elect, to be loved by God. How beautiful! How wonderful.

Wait a second!

What about those who are at the "other" place? When they are in eternal torment, they will also read "Chosen to be here from the foundation of the world". Huh? I am in this torment ONLY because God didn't elect me? Why did I even go to the "Great White Throne Judgment"? How could I be judged by God, while the whole time the responsibility was on HIM to elect me? Shouldn't God be judging Himself?

Election (Calvinism) teaches that all believers are elected by God. That man has no say in determining his own salvation. What is the point of the judgment seats if this were really the case? Who did Jesus die for—the elect *only?* Is faith the gift of God? Who are the elect of the Bible? Why do people believe in election? These are some of the questions that will be analyzed and answered using scripture and logic.

The Bible says, "The Lord is not slack concerning his promise, as some men count slackness; but is longsuffering to us-ward, not willing that ANY should perish, but that ALL should come to repentance" (2 Pet 3:9).

Logic says: If God wants ALL to come to repentance (a change of mind), why did He only elect to save a few?

Calvinists/Electionists believe that God only died for the elect. The pastor at a church I was attending stated, "God hates sin and He hates the sinner." I cannot remember the verse he used. He did use hell as an example of how God hates the sinner. Man... how lucky you are to be elected by God, knowing that Jesus died for you (the elect).

What does the Bible say?

The Bible says "...he is the propitiation for our sins: and not for ours only, but also for the sins of the **whole world**" (1 John 2:2).

The Bible says, "The next day John seeth Jesus coming unto him, and saith, 'Behold the Lamb of God, which taketh away the sin of **the world**'" (John 1:29).

The Bible says, "This is good, and pleases God our Savior, who wants **all people** to be saved and to come to a knowledge of the truth" (I Tim 2:3,4).

The Bible says, "But we see Jesus, who was made a little lower than the angels for the suffering of death, crowned with glory and honour; that he by the grace of God should taste death for **every man**" (Heb 2:9).

Logic says, "Do the words 'all', 'every', and 'world' mean 'elect'?"

Calvinists/Electionists believe that faith is a gift from God. They believe mankind is totally depraved, that a man cannot make any choices on his own. Ephesians 2:8,9 reads, "For by grace ye are saved through faith, it is not of yourselves, it is the gift of God." By reading this verse, Calvinists/Electionists say that faith is the gift of God. Some even claim that "faith" is a work, therefore people cannot have faith on their own.

The Bible says, "For the wages of sin is death; but the gift of God **IS** eternal life through Jesus Christ our Lord" (Rom 6:23).

The Bible says, "But for the one that worketh not, but believeth on the one who justifies the ungodly, his faith is counted as righteousness" (Rom 4:5). Paul **clearly** separates works and faith.

Logic says, "If a man cannot have faith on his own, how can the unsaved have faith in Allah, Buddha, evolution, or even his own works?"

Also, check your Bibles and look to see how many times Jesus rebuked His disciples for having little faith. Some examples are found in Matthew 6:30; 8:26; 14:31; 16:8 and Mark 4:40. IF faith were the gift of God and God grants levels of faith, shouldn't Jesus have rebuked the Father and Himself for **not** giving them enough faith? Shouldn't Jesus have apologized and said, "Oh, my bad, I need to give you more faith"?

Why do Calvinists/Electionists believe that all Christians are elected? Where in the Bible does it mention God elected those who would be saved? Let's take a look at a few of those verses, shall we? John 6:44 reads, "No man come to me except the Father which hath sent me draw him". WOW. There you have it! God has to draw you to Him. See, we are elected. This makes sense. However, what else does the Bible say?

The Bible says, "And I, if I be lifted up, will draw **ALL men** to me" (John 12:32).

Logic says, "What is the definition of 'all'? Did it say 'all elect'?"

How does God draw all men? He does so through the gospel and the Holy Spirit. We read in Romans 1:16, "For I am not ashamed of the gospel of Christ: for it is the POWER of God unto salvation **to everyone** that believeth." In Acts 8:29, we also see that the Spirit spoke to Philip.

We will not review all the passages the Calvinists/ Electionists use to support their theology. This chapter would be fifty pages long if we did. However, let us now take a look at Romans 9:1-24 in some depth. In this passage you will see:

> "For the children being not yet born, neither having done any good or evil that the purpose of God according to election might stand, not of works, but of him that calleth; and that God will save whom he will save."

By themselves, these passages clearly teach election. Let's take a look at the **whole** passage. In the first few verses Paul's heart is heavy. He is hoping that his own people (ISRAEL) would come to repentance (change of mind). The law was given to them. The covenant of Abraham, all the promises, the Messiah! Israel was elected by God. Deuteronomy 7:6 says,

> "For you are a people holy to the Lord your God. The Lord your God has chosen you out of all the peoples on the face of the earth to be his people, his treasured possession."

Paul begins to go through the lineage and Old Testament scripture. This was very early in the Covenant made with Israel (Paul is still addressing his concern for the elected nation). He then brings up the Old Testament of Esau and Jacob, still referring to nations.

> "And the LORD said unto her, 'Two **nations** are in thy womb, and two manner of people shall be sepa-rated from thy bowels; and the one people shall be stronger than the other people; and the elder shall serve the younger'" (Gen 25:23).

Paul begins to talk about God. Is He unrighteous? He will have mercy on whom He will have mercy. Bringing glory to God through power, wrath and mercy. Verse 24 – including the **gentiles** apart from the ELECTED Israel. In verses 20 and 21. They should not say to God, why hast thou made me like this? He references the potter and the clay.

> "'O house of **ISRAEL**, cannot I do with you as this potter?' saith the LORD. 'Behold, as the clay is in the potter's hand, so are ye in mine hand, O house of **ISRAEL**" (Jeremiah 18:6).

If you read and understand the context of Romans 9, you can clearly see that this passage is about the elected Israel. Much of Israel rejected their Messiah. As a result of their unbelief, God hardened their hearts. Romans 9 has nothing to do with individual salvation—nothing whatsoever. Here is where we go from whatsoever to whosoever. **Whosoever** is a word that appears many times in the Bible. Since we know that God is not a respecter of persons, and we also know the Bible is the word of God, let's take a look at a few scriptures.

The Bible says, "For **whosoever** shall call upon the name of the Lord shall be saved" (Rom 10:13).

The Bible says, "And it shall come to pass, that **whosoever** shall call on the name of the Lord shall be saved" (Acts 2:21).

The Bible says, "And let him that is athirst come. And **whosoever** will, let him take the water of life freely" (Rev 21:17).

The Bible says, "For God so loved the world, that he gave his only begotten Son, that **whosoever** believeth in him should not perish, but have everlasting life" (John 3:16).

OK, this is the last one, I promise. Calvinists/Electionists use Ephesians 1:4, which reads, "According as he hath chosen us in him before the foundation of the world, that we should be holy and without blame before him in love." There you have it—chosen from the foundation of the world. Forget everything else in the Bible (world, all, every, whosoever, rejected and believed; etc). I cannot deny election is in the Bible. It is—*but who is elected/predestined?*

- Israel was elected
- Jesus was elected to be the sacrifice for mankind before the foundation of the world
- Angels are elected to minister, worship, etc.

Does this mean that Christians were elected/predestined? God forbid! (Incorporating Paul there.) The *plan* of salvation was predestined. The plan, you ask? Whosoever believed would be saved. Once saved, the Christians (*whomever* they might be) are predestined for holy living (Eph 1:4). The Christian was predestined to do good works (not necessary for salvation). God doesn't elect unto Christianity, He elects from Christianity. God chose, from the foundation of the world, to save whosoever would believe **in Him**. Calvinists/Electionists put the cart WAY ahead of the horse. They misinterpret scripture (as we all can do) to fit their doctrine.

Through the scriptures, we can clearly see that predestination/election unto salvation is incorrect. It is offered to **every man, to all, to whosoever, to the world**. I refuse to believe (with much biblical evidence) that my God would elect people to go to hell. He is not cruel. God asked Moses, "How long will it be ere they believe in me?" (Numbers 14:11). "Satan blinds the minds of those who believe not" (2 Cor 4:4). "Ye will not come unto me that ye may have life" (John 5:40). People can't refuse to believe if they don't have a choice! Satan can't blind those who are "chosen from the foundation of the world" to go to hell. They would be blinded without Satan's help! How can people "refuse" not to come to Him if they don't have a choice? I again am reminded of the most popular verse in the Bible, John 3:16:

"For God so loved the elect, that he gave His only begotten Son, that whomsoever He chooses, shall have everlasting life" (obvious sarcasm here).

God does choose who gets eternal life. He chose, from the foundation of the world, the plan for salvation—the predestined plan that whosoever believeth in Him shall have everlasting life. Why? Because God so loved **THE WORLD**.

Chapter 23

Why the Bible?

———∽∾∽———

Although this chapter does not flow within the context of this book, I decided to put it in to help grow your faith in the Bible itself. IF you are trying to spread the good news of the gospel, you will inevitably run into someone who has no belief in the Bible whatsoever. As a result, you need to have reasons why you believe the Bible to be from God. An answer similar to "I don't know, I just believe" will probably not help your cause with a non-Bible believer. The following are logical reasons why I believe the Bible to be from God.

1. NEW TESTAMENT ACCURATE AS A HISTORICAL DOCUMENT

University Professor Bruce Metzger of Princeton University analyzed, determined, and was **quoted** as saying that the New Testament had a minimum accuracy of 99.6% as a historical translated document ONLY. No other document has that kind of accuracy due to human error/perspective. The remaining 0.4% was not disproven or a translation error. Other scholars include: Westcott and Hort – 98.3%;

Ezra Abbott 99.75 %; A.T. Robertson (greek scholar) – 99.9% I believe only AT Robertson, of these scholars, MIGHT have been Christian.

2. THE BIBLE HAS STOOD A MAJOR TEST

Since its inception, the Bible has been analyzed, scrutinized, beaten and tested. It has yet to be disproven. For example, I recently debated the Bible with a Muslim. He gave me ten contradictions in the Bible. Within an hour I could answer seven of them (and I am no scholar). For hundreds and hundreds of years, the Bible has stood a major test—it has stood the test of TIME. One would think after this many years and that much scrutiny; it would have been disproven by now. There is an extremely high probability, because of ALL the dissection and investigation that the Bible would have been completely dismissed by 2013. It still stands without being disproved – it has withstood the TEST of time.

3. THE AMOUNT OF AUTHORS **INCREASES PROBABILITY** OF DIVINE SUPPORT

The Bible has 44 different authors. If the Bible cannot be disproven over hundreds and hundreds of years and was written by 44 different people, something of the supernatural had to be guiding them. For example, if a thief ran into a room with ten people in it, stole a purse, and quickly ran out, you would get eight different descriptions of the robber. WHY does this happen? Human perspective. There would be different perspectives on height, weight, jacket color, etc. (This is proven to be true.) Because the Bible has 44 authors and was written over thousands of years, the amount of errors SHOULD be very numerous (based on human error and probability)! However, it has not been disproven. This is not HUMANLY POSSIBLE!

4. THE BIBLE PREDICTS THE FUTURE OVER AND OVER AGAIN

Bible prophecy takes the book from a MUST read to the SUPERNATURAL. At least 20% of the Bible is prophetic in nature. It is humanly IMPOSSIBLE to predict the future hundreds or even thousands of years in advance. The Bible DOES this and has **_NEVER_** been wrong. There are many prophecy points that the Bible predicts. They concern Jesus, Israel, world governments, and end times. I could write a 50-page paper on this, but will attempt to keep it much shorter.

- The Bible predicted the death of the Jesus, TO THE YEAR, 550 years before Jesus was crucified. It might be to the day – one would have to study a little astronomy. Jesus fulfilled at least 20 Old Testament prophecies of the coming Messiah (i.e. Born in Bethlehem, would be a Nazareen, sold out for 30 pieces of silver, buried in a rich mans tomb, bruised for our iniquities, entering the city on a donkey, etc.). A mathematician stated that to fulfill only 8 of them with the amount of people on the earth meant the chances were 10 to the 17th power. That is 1 in 1,000,000,000,000,000,000. What is that number called, a mega-zillion? If that's the chances with eight prophecies, what's the number for 20 fulfilled prophecies?

- The Bible foretold Israel becoming an INDEPENDENT nation in 1948 TO THE YEAR. It prophesied this 2,500 years ago. This disproves anyone that says prophecy was written after the event occurred. The Bible was written WELL before 1948. Not to mention archeology has proven when each book was actually written.
- World governments were predicted: Babylon, Medes-Persians, Greece and Rome.
- Greece was predicted 250 years prior to Alexander the Great. It is historically documented that he died an early death and that the land was divided among his four generals. The Bible predicted that Greece would not only rule, but that the kingdom would be divided by four – 250 years prior!
- End times prophecy over the last hundred years predicted over 1,900 years ago; below are just a couple:
  ○ Man would be traveling to and fro throughout the world. Until the last hundred years, everyone was on horseback. Today people are traveling in cars, trains, airplanes, etc.
  ○ Man would be capable of destroying every living person – until the last ½ century, man used guns and swords for war. Today we have nuclear, biological and chemical weapons capable of wiping out the human race several times over.
  ○ One that hasn't happened yet but interesting – in the Old Testament (the book of Daniel) the antichrist will cause the sacrifices of Israel to cease. For this to happen 2,500 years later, there needs to be a Jewish temple built. *Today* Israel wants

a temple to be built and the rabbis are being trained how to sacrifice animals properly. This ceasing of sacrifices happens in the middle of the last seven years of the age. It looks like we are getting close.

SUMMARY —It is impossible for man to predict the future without divine help. The Bible has much more prophesy than this. These are only a few examples. **THE BIBLE IS OF THE SUPERNATURAL!**

5. THE HUMAN BEHAVIOR OF THE APOSTLES SHOWS THAT JESUS WAS RESURRECTED

Most of the apostles/disciples were murdered for their faith. Many of them suffered horrible deaths to include crucifixion, beheading, being stoned to death and being speared to death. The Bible only tells of one of their deaths. There is valid **historical data** supporting how the others died. All they would have had to do to live was to deny Jesus. They couldn't do it. Why? They saw His sinless nature, His divine miracles and His RESURRECTION from the dead. It has been argued that they were lying and it was all made up. Well, who do you know that would die a horrible death *for a lie?* There are NO living humans who would die for something they **KNEW** was not true. People die for a lie all the time (suicide bombers), however they **BELIEVE** that lie to be true. Most of the disciples wouldn't attend the crucifixion. They were miserable. One of the disciples (Thomas) wouldn't believe Jesus rose from the dead until he literally saw Him (even though others saw Him previously).

However, when they saw Jesus RESURRECTED from the dead, they were willing to tell the world and die horrible deaths to proclaim the "good news" of Jesus Christ. WHY were they willing to die? They witnessed it! Again, there is valid historical data concerning their deaths (only one in the Bible).

SUMMARY – No human dies like this for a known lie. They were able to endure horrible deaths because of what they literally saw with their OWN eyes. This gives more validity to the Bible from a human behavioral perspective.

6. GOT TO LOVE THE FINDINGS OF SCIENCE (Bible verses written from 2000 BC to 500 BC)

  a. After Columbus, we discovered the earth was round. The Bible states, "It is he that sitteth upon the CIRCLE of the earth, and the inhabitants thereof are as grasshoppers; that stretcheth out the heavens as a curtain, and spreadeth them out as a tent to dwell in" (Isa 40:22).

  b. For years ATLAS or an elephant held up the earth. Later we discovered it was some kind of gravitational pull. The Bible states, "He stretcheth out the north over the empty place, and hangeth the earth upon nothing" (Job 26: 7).

  c. Until meteorologists had the technology to capture the winds' circular motion, wind direction was unknown. The Bible states, "The wind goeth toward the south, and turneth about unto the north; it whirleth about continually, and the wind returneth again according to his circuits" (Ecc 1:6).

d. Scientists have recently discovered that life is contained in the blood. The Bible stated 3,500 years ago, "For the life of a creature is in the blood, and I have given it to you to make atonement for yourselves on the altar; it is the blood that makes atonement for one's life" (Lev 17:11).

SUMMARY – these are a few examples from the Bible that relate to Science. The book already told us things that apparently took us a few thousand years to discover. When will we learn?

Chapter 24

The Gospel revisited

—◊◊◊—

As already stated earlier, this book will start and end with "the gospel". There has been a little more written in this chapter versus the first gospel chapter. The verses presented here are CLEAR. They can't possibly be taken to mean "something else". The Bible, being the word of God CANNOT contradict itself.

> "For I am not ashamed of the **GOSPEL** of Christ: for it is the power of God unto salvation to everyone that **BELIEVETH."**

What is the gospel according to the Bible? I mean, since IT IS the power of God unto salvation to whoever believes it. The gospel is **DECLARED** in 1 Corinthians.

> Moreover, brethren, I **DECLARE** unto you the **GOSPEL** which I preached unto you, which also ye have received, and wherein ye stand; By which also ye are saved..... how that Christ **DIED FOR OUR SINS**

according to the scriptures; And that he was buried, and that he rose again the third day according to the scriptures. (1 Cor 15:1,2,4)

What happens when someone believes/trusts that Jesus (God in the flesh) **DIED FOR OUR SINS** and rose from the dead? The answer is in Ephesians.

"In whom ye also **TRUSTED**, after that ye heard the word of truth, the **GOSPEL** of your salvation: in whom also after that ye **BELIEVED**, ye were **SEALED** with that Holy Spirit of promise" (Eph 1:13).

We see that people believe (put TOTAL confidence in; trusts; relies upon) this **GOSPEL,** that Jesus "died for **THEIR** sins", they are **SEALED** by the Holy Spirit. One can never be unsealed. One is sealed until the day of redemption.

"...and grieve not the Holy Spirit whereby ye **ARE SEALED** unto the day of redemption" (Eph 4:30).

Simply to clarify from a different angle, how many sins did Jesus die for (pay for)? The Bible is clear. Jesus died for **ALL** of them.

"And you, being dead in your sins and the uncircum-cision of your flesh, hath he quickened together with him, having **FORGIVEN YOU ALL TRESPASSES**; blotting out the handwriting of ordinances that was against us, which was contrary to us, and took it out of the way, nailing it to his cross" (Col 2:13,14).

"And by him all that believe are justified from **ALL THINGS**, from which ye could not be justified by the law of Moses" (Acts 13:39).

OK. There should be no question as to what these verses read. It's pretty clear. They can't be taken any other way. Now I would like to translate this into a worldly example. This has helped others in the past.

"For the wages of sin is death, but the **GIFT** of God is eternal life through Jesus Christ our Lord" (Romans 6:23).

This verse is sending two clear messages. First, notice salvation is a GIFT. Pssst, a little secret for you: gifts are FREE! Second is what we owe for our sin. Wages is a term mostly used for employment. Wages are what are owed to the employee in exchange for the work he or she has done. Well death is what we owe in exchange for our sin. Death, in this passage, can refer to physical death or the second death, which is eternal torment in a literal lake of fire that burns forever (see Rev 20:14). "The wages of sin is death." So, let's ask ourselves a few questions, shall we?

If you had 10 chocolate bars and you gave away ALL 10 bars, how many bars would you have left? The answer: **NONE.**

If you had 25 mugs at a yard sale and someone bought ALL 25 mugs, how many mugs would you have left? The answer: **NONE**

If you had $100 and a thief stole ALL $100, how many dollars would you have left? The answer: **NONE**

HERE IT COMES!

If you have ALL these sins you owe as wages and JESUS came and paid for ALL those sins, how many sins would you have left to send you to hell? The answer: **NONE**.

Yes folks, it is that simple. Jesus died to pay for **ALL** your sins. This is the gospel (the Good News). All you must do is believe it. The moment you do, you **are sealed** by the Holy Spirit unto the day of redemption. LISTEN CAREFULLY, just in case you did NOT catch it while reading this book. Have YOU believed this gospel? Have YOU been justified? Have YOU been washed as white as snow? In other words, do YOU KNOW for a FACT where you are going when you die? Is 100% of your faith in the gospel of Jesus? IF so, you are going to heaven when you die. Your soul can "rest".

OR

Are YOU still seeking to be justified? Are YOU hoping to be good enough to "earn" heaven? Are YOU trusting in the LAW (repent of sins) to save you? Are YOU thinking that YOU have anything to do with going to heaven other than to believe the gospel? Have YOU been FOOLED by religion? IF so, I am extremely concerned for you. You are probably going to spend eternity **IN THE LAKE OF FIRE**. This book was written for YOU in mind. I say "probably" as it is possible that at one point, your faith was in Christ, you were saved. Sometime afterward, religion got to you.There is **NO** other gospel **THEN** the gospel **DECLARED** in 1 Corinthians 15:1-4.

> I marvel that ye are so soon removed from him that called you into the grace of Christ unto **ANOTHER GOSPEL**: Which is not another; but there be some that trouble you, and would PERVERT the gospel of Christ. But though we, or an angel from heaven,

PREACH ANY OTHER GOSPEL unto you than that which we have preached unto you, **let him be accursed**. (Galatians 1:6-8)

IF **YOU** have **NOT** truly trusted Him yet, would you trust Him now? Jesus did **ALL** the work to provide you with salvation. Will you trust (believe) that Jesus **DIED FOR ALL YOUR SINS** and rose again? Will you dismiss the "religions of DO" and **REST** in Him who says "**DONE**"? In the famous last words of Jesus on the cross, "**IT IS FINISHED**"!

Chapter 25

Closing Thoughts

———꿰꿰———

I have found, through my many hours of study, debate and discussion, most of professing Christianity will **PROBABLY NOT** be going to heaven when they die. This is quite simply, extremely disturbing. We are talking about spending eternity in a **LITERAL Lake of Fire**. Think about that for a few seconds. **EVERYONE** who has **NEVER** believed in the gospel **ALONE**, that you know, is going to spend **FOREVER** in a lake of fire. There is **no** escape. There is **no** hope of getting out. They will be there **FOREVER**. This is pretty sad when one considers salvation from hell was **FREE, a GIFT**. Why does anyone go to hell? I can really only come up with two answers to this question.

1. Most don't believe Jesus died for their sins. They don't believe Jesus did this for them. (This includes most people.) They do not accept the payment He made on the cross.

2. Most don't believe Jesus's sacrifice on the cross was good enough. (This includes **most** of professing

Christianity). They do not accept that His payment was sufficient.

Everyone falls into one of these two categories. Although everyone going to hell falls under the first, I thought it a good idea to add the second when talking about the religious. The **religious** will always add to the cross. Whether they are adding sacraments, works, church affiliation, the law (repent of sins) or themselves to the plan of salvation, their mantra will always be "DO" to go to heaven. However, Jesus says "done". He did all the work necessary for everyone's salvation. One simply needs to believe, trust, put confidence in, who Jesus was (God's only Son; God in the flesh) and what He did on the cross (Jesus died for **YOUR** sins and rose again).

That's it! It is that simple. Does the KING JAMES VERSION call it simple? Yes, it does. "But I fear, lest by any means, as the serpent beguiled Eve through his subtilty, so your minds should be corrupted from the **SIMPLICITY** that is in Christ. For if he that cometh preacheth another Jesus, whom we have not preached, or if ye receive another spirit, which ye have not received, or another gospel, which ye have not accepted, ye might well bear with him" (2 Cor 11:3, 4).

There is **NO other Jesus** and there is **NO other gospel**.

The goals of this book are many.

1. I hope that it was an easy read. I am not a great writer. As Paul put it, I don't come with excellent speech. However, I do pray it was clear from your perspective.

2. IF you have never TRULY put your faith in the true GOSPEL of Jesus, my sincere hope is that you would. Religion has a way of getting people to put faith in

works and the law to go to heaven. But, Jesus wants you to put 100% of your faith IN HIM. When you do, He promised NEVER to cast you out, NEVER to lose you; and NOTHING will pluck you from His hand.

3. IF you have trusted in the gospel of Jesus alone for salvation, you are going to heaven. But maybe, you have gotten caught up in "religion". Maybe, you have become one of the "religious". This same thing happened to the Galatians. I have heard the term "Galatianism". Religion infected the church of Galatia by removing them from the gospel. I hope this book has gotten you back on track to believing and proclaiming a clear gospel message to others.

4. IF you have trusted in the gospel of Jesus alone for salvation, you are going to heaven. But maybe religion has confused you and you began to doubt your salvation, I hope this book increased your faith. I know that as soon as I could explain those passages that seemed to contradict, my faith grew. If this is you, hopefully your confidence has increased (or been restored).
Heb 10:35—Cast not away therefore your confidence, which hath great recompense of REWARD.

5. IF you are currently a believer in the gospel and you are not doubting or wavering in your salvation due to religion, I hope this book was an interesting read. Maybe you can share it with someone who has not believed the gospel yet. Hopefully there was a passage or two that was explained and you got what I like to call, "a nugget".

Paul, when writing to the carnal church at Corinth (1 Cor 3:1-3) **after** they were saved (Acts 18:1), he had many things to tell them about what they **should** be doing since they were already saved. Before he got into these things, Paul wrote this...

> For Christ sent me not to baptize, but to **preach the gospel**: not with wisdom of words, lest the cross of Christ should be made of none effect. For the preaching of the cross is to them that perish foolishness; but unto us which **are saved** it is the power of God. But **we preach Christ crucified**, unto the Jews a stumblingblock, and unto the Greeks foolishness; And I, brethren, when I came to you, came not with excellency of speech or of wisdom, declaring unto you the testimony of God. For I determined **NOT TO KNOW ANYTHING** among you, save **Jesus Christ, and him crucified**. (1 Cor 1:17,18; 1 Cor 1:23; 1 Cor 2:1,2)

Did you catch it? Paul didn't care to know anything about them (an unsaved person) except Jesus and Him crucified (the gospel). **I DON'T CARE** about your background. **I DON'T CARE** what sins you have committed. **I DON'T CARE** what religion you are into today. **I DON'T CARE** what "Christian" denomination you are a member of currently. **I ONLY CARE** to know that you have **believed** (trusted) in the gospel ALONE (not to know anything else about you).

What, then, are we to do after believing this gospel and being sealed forever? That would be a completely different book. I can reference the chapter of "should do" as well as the same book written to the carnal church at Corinth.

According to the grace of God which is given unto me, as a wise master builder, I have laid the foundation, and another buildeth thereon. But let every man take heed how he buildeth thereupon. FOR OTHER FOUNDATION CAN NO MAN LAY THAN THAT IS LAID, **WHICH IS JESUS CHRIST**. Now if any man build upon THIS foundation gold, silver, precious stones, wood, hay, stubble; Every man's work shall be made manifest: for the day shall declare it, because it shall be revealed by fire; and the fire shall try every man's work of what sort it is. If any man's work abide which he hath built thereupon, he shall receive a **reward**. If any man's work shall be burned, he shall suffer loss: but he himself shall be saved; yet so as by fire. (1 Cor 3:10-15)

There are REWARDS for the believer who chooses to serve Jesus. Salvation is free. Rewards are earned. Notice verse 11. The foundation is Jesus. The foundation is NOT...

1. (not) Jesus AND the law
2. (not) Jesus AND works
3. (not) Jesus AND sacraments
4. (not) Jesus AND yourself
5. (not) Jesus AND church affiliation.

The foundation is Jesus Christ alone. How do you get on this foundation? By believing in whom Jesus was (Gods only Son; God in the flesh) and what He did for YOU at the cross (the gospel)! **He died for YOU.** He died to pay for **ALL** your sins. Are you on this foundation or one of the false "religious" foundations listed above? Your eternal destiny depends on it!

The opening exercise revisited.

Ask yourself these two questions and write down your answer on a piece of paper.

1. Do I KNOW where I am going when I die?
2. Why or why not?

Look at the answer you wrote down! This answer will tell yourself directly what your faith is **REALLY** in to go to heaven. I hope it is in Jesus and **nothing else**.

God Bless. I truly hope to see you all in heaven one day. I know where I am going when I die. I have **NO SINS** to send me to hell. Jesus died for **ALL** of my sins and I BELIEVE it. Remember, **IT IS A FREE GIFT!** Accept the free gift by faith and **KNOW** you have eternal life.

"These things have I written unto you that BELIEVE (or trust) on the name of the Son of God; that ye may **KNOW** that ye have eternal life, and that ye may believe on the name of the Son of God" (1 John 5:13).

NOTES

1. There is ZERO intent to profit by the sale of this book. It was written with the purposes previously listed and money was NOT one of those purposes. All profits, if any, will be donated unless a catastrophic event occurs within my family. I am not here to "make merchandise" of the saints.
2. Anyone can email me at simplesinner8@gmail.com with questions or comments. IF I do not respond something has happened to the email account or I went home.
3. One quote from Ron Shea; cleargospel.org (fruit inspectors)
4. Ralph Yankee Arnold on YouTube. I HIGHLY recommend him.
5. Although not on YouTube, I also recommend Tom Cucuzza from Northland Baptist church in MN. His sermons are on-line through his church website.
6. Once you see that many are believing (trusting) in "another gospel" and you are looking for some kind of fellowship with like minded believers to help grow your faith. I recommend expreacherman.com.
7. PLEASE be good bereans verify ALL scripture used (including parentheses) in the **KJV Bible**.

CPSIA information can be obtained
at www.ICGtesting.com
Printed in the USA
BVHW070016011122
650615BV00003B/7